Borderland BIRDS

Nesting Birds of The Southern Border

ROLAND H. WAUER

To order additional copies of this book, contact:
Xlibris
1-888-795-4274
www.Xlibris.com
Orders@Xlibris.com

ISBN: Softcover   978-1-9845-8793-0
       Hardcover   978-1-9845-8794-7
       EBook   978-1-9845-8792-3

Library of Congress Control Number: 2020913204

Print information available on the last page

Rev. date: 07/31/2020

CONTENTS

DEDICATION

To Betty Wauer
We shared many birding adventures

INTRODUCTION

There are several dozen U. S. birds that occur only along the southern edge of the country. Many of these are Mexican species that reach the U. S. at the northernmost edge of their range. And because of these "specialties," they become target birds for those of us wanted to see them all in the United States.

For example, Mexico has provided us with such borderland species as masked duck, red-billed pigeon, white-tipped dove, hook-billed kite, aplomado falcon, whiskered screech-owl, elegant trogon, common pauraque; the magnificent, blue-throated, and lucifer hummingbirds; great kiskadee, northern beardless-flycatcher, Altamira oriole, yellow-eyed junco, and many others.

It is possible that the number of recent and/or "new" members of the U.S. avifauna will increase in the future, although introductions of new species are doubtful. However, the effects of global warming are likely to result in numerous avifaunal changes. These can include both increases as well as declines.

New breeding species due to global warming and a resultant northward shifts into changing conditions necessary for their livelihood include wild Muscovy and masked ducks, crane and roadside hawks, northern jacana, mangrove cuckoo, mottled owl, tawny-collared nightjar, plain-capped starthroat, mountain trogon, Amazon kingfisher, bronze-winged woodpecker; tufted, pine, and Nutting's flycatchers; masked tityra, Sinaloa and gray-breasted martins, spot-breasted wren, black-capped gnatcatcher, brown-backed solitaire, Aztec thrush, blue mockingbird, gray silky-flycatcher, yellow-green vireo, gray-crowned yellowthroat, slate-throated redstart, fan-tailed and golden-crowned warblers, flame-colored tanager, crimson-collared and yellow grosbeaks, blue bunting, yellow-faced grassquit, black-vented and streak-backed orioles, and black-headed siskin.

A few of these have already visited the U.S. over the years, but so far have not been documented as nesting.

LIST OF ILLUSTRATIONS

ACKNOWLEDGEMENTS

Includes all who accompanied me or provided assistance.

John and Kendra Abbott, Mark Adams, C. Phillip Allen, Keith Arnold, John Arvin, John Baccus, John Baker, Jon Barlow, Sharon Bartels, Dominic Bartol, Ben Basham, Bob Behrstock, Anne Bellamy, John Bissonette, W. Frank Blair, Andre Blanchard, Jim Booker, J. R. Bloomberg, Carolyn Borden, Bill Bourbon, Jim Brock, Hank and Pricilla Brodkin, Kelly Bryan, George Burdick, Byron Burger, Bob Burleson, Dennis Carter, Will Carter, Alan Chaney, Bill Clark, Herb Clark, Jim Court, David and Jan Dauphin, Victor Davila, Shannon Davies, Don Davis, Bill Degenhart, James Dick, Larry Ditto, Chris Durden, Dave Easterla, Mark and Maryann Eastman, Doug Eddelman, Mark Elwonger, Victor Emanual, Doug Evans, Eric and Sally Finkelstein, Mike Fleming, Mark Flippo, Brush Freeman, Rene Flores, Ned Fritz, Craig Farquhar, John Galley, Charles and Louise Gambill, Fred Gehlbach, Paul Gerrish, Jeff Glassberg, Bill Graber, Byron Griffin, Dan Hardy, Dave Hanson, Allan Haygood, Frank Hedges, David Henderson, O. R. Henderson, Wes Hendrik, Houston Holder, P. D. Hulse, Clark Hubbs, Charles and Alice Hunt, C. L. Husmann, Grainger Hunt, Jimmy Jackson, Pauline James, Cheryl Johnson, R. Roy Johnson, Clyde Jones, Ted Jones, Frank Judd, Paul Julian, Walt Kittams, Mark Kopeny, Paul Krausmann, Joe Kuban, Jim Lane, Greg Lasley, Anne LeSassier, David Ligon, Bill Lindemann, Rick LoBello, Glenn Lowe, Jr., David Marshall, Joe and Elsie Marshall, Roy McBride, Wayne and Martha McAllister, Terry Maxwell, Nancy McGowan, Bonnie McKinney, Bill Millstead, Paul Miliotis, Steve Moore, Bruce Moorhead, Derek Muschalek, Dick Nelson, Bill and LeeAnn Nichols, Dale Nichols, Rob Norton, Andy O'Neil, Frank Oberhansley, Paul Opler, Brent Ortego, Noberto Ortega, Mike Overton, Paul and Nancy Palmer, Mike Parmeter, Jim Petersen, Fr. Thomas

Pincelli, Jeff Pippen, Allan Phillips, Warren Pulich, Mike Quinn, Dick Rasp, Janet Rathjen, Bill Reid, Martin Reid, Peter Reisz, Van Remsen, Barbara Ribble, Cecile Riley, David Riskind, William and Alice Roe, Rose Ann Rowlett, Kent Rylander, C. L. Sachett, Jr., David Schmidly, Chuck Sexton, Norm Scott, Peter Scott, George Seaman, Willie Sekula, Chuck Sexton, Bill Schaldach, Jim Scudday, Jim Shiflett, Roger Siglin, Ray Skiles, Fred Sladen, Arnold Small, Ruth Snyder, Hope Spear, Jerry and Nancy Strickland, Lowell Sumner, Jim and Cilla Tucker, Mike Turner, John and Gloria Tveten, Tom Urban, Arnold VanPelt, Barbara Volkle, Gary Waggerman, Betty Wauer, Brent Wauer, Jim and Lynne Weber, Ralph and Buddy Wells, Brian Wheeler, Paul Whitson, Sue Wiedenfeld, Francis Williams, Anse Windham, David Wolf, Mimi Hope Wolf, Bo and Woody West, Keith Yarborough, Lee Ziegler, Albin Zeitel, and Barry Zimmer.

The following additional folks provided photographs to illustrate the various species and their habitats.

The majority of photographs were provided by Greg Lasley; he has constantly responded to my requests. Other photographers who provided images include (alphabetically) Bob Behrstock, Kelly Bryan, Martin Reid, and Betty Wauer.

Borderland Birds in AOU Order

The following annotated list of borderland birds are currently known to nest in the U.S. Most are known only for the southwestern states of Arizona, New Mexico, and Texas.

MASKED DUCK

The masked duck is a tropical species that is not only rare in occurrence, but is elusive and shy, as well. It is similar in appearance to the ruddy duck; it is in fact the same genus: *Oxyura*. The major difference in appearance between the two species is the more extensive white cheeks of the ruddy duck compared to the black cheeks of the masked duck. Also, ruddy ducks usually are found in open water, while masked ducks prefer the edges of ponds close to vegetation and rarely venture too far away from easy cover and shelter. Masked ducks are very secretive in nature, usually skulking and hard to see. They may merge into open water at night to feed. And they rarely associate with other ducks; they usually are quiet, although they are known to make low grunts.

Steve Howell and Sophie Webb, however, mentioned their voice in *A Guide to the Birds of Mexico and Northern Central America*, thusly: "male rarely gives a throaty *oo-oo-oo* or *kit-roo-kirroo-kiroo*, female a short, repeated hiss."

One of the "stiff-tailed" ducks, masked ducks are native from Mexico to South America as well as several of the Caribbean islands. Although they are not migrants, they do move about a good deal. Their take-off from the water is nearly vertical like dabbling ducks.

In the U.S., masked ducks occur only rarely along the Mexican border and in Florida. They frequent small freshwater ponds with marshy vegetation and surrounding tree cover, as well as mangroves and even rice paddies. Their diet consists of aquatic vegetation such as smartweeds, sedges, grasses and other aquatic plants as well as insects and crustacea. All their foods are acquired by diving.

In Texas, masked ducks are erratic in occurrence, and only in the Lower Rio Grande Valley. According to Timothy Brush, in *Nesting Birds of a Tropical Frontier*, they are seen in small numbers only in wet years and only in the upper and central Texas coast regions. Brush wrote that:

> Masked ducks move around as pond quality changes. Individuals may appear on once-dry ponds that have just been filled naturally or artificially. For example, on April 5, 1996, I saw a male in breeding plumage on Santa Ana's Cattail Lake, which had been dry the previous winter and early spring. Habitat conditions were important in June and July of 1995; three Masked

Ducks resided regularly on Willow Lake at Santa Ana. The lake was drained when at least 75 percent was covered with cattails…Masked ducks prefer ponds with yellow lotus, yellow waterlily, and water hyacinth, but flooded huisache and sesbania may be used also.

Although there are only a few documented nesting masked ducks in recent years in the U.S., courting males have been reported as rising their tails and lowering their bills onto their chests while making soft calls and making short rushes across the surface of ponds. Nests are a woven bowl of reeds and grasses, and are built only by the female.

In Mexico, masked ducks occur along the Gulf Coastal Plain and along the Pacific Slope from Sinaloa to Colima. Their range extends to south Peru and northern Argentina.

PLAIN CHACHALACA

Anyone visiting Bentsen-Rio Grande Valley State Park or Santa Ana National Wildlife Refuge, both located in the Lower Rio Grande Valley of Texas, will undoubtedly become acquainted with chachalacas. And anyone who camps overnight almost anywhere along the Lower Rio Grande, will certainly be awakened by their loud and obnoxious dawn songs. They even duet with their neighbors; the chorus usually continues until daylight. Timothy Brush, a local Valley resident, wrote in *Nesting Birds of a Tropical Frontier*, that their "ear-splitting chant can be heard hundreds of yards away and definitely underscores the tropical feel of the Valley. Once one pair (or group) starts singing, others pick up the beat, until the woods resound with chachalaca noise."

And Kent Rylander, in *The Behavior of Texas Birds*, provided yet another comment on their voice:

> Unchallenged as one of our noisiest birds, especially during the breeding season. Call: delivered from a perch in a tall tree, a loud, resonant, penetrating *cha lac*. Birds sing mainly at dawn and at dusk and before thunderstorms. One bird imitates the call, but as neighbors join in, the event quickly cascades into a disorganized, frenzied chorus. They also utter a *kak kak* when alarmed. The male's deeper voice has been attributed to his looped trachea.

The plain chachalaca is a large bird with a long tail and long, stout legs. It has a wingspan of about 26 inches, yet it spends the majority of its time on the ground or in trees. Although the plain chachalaca is well illustrated in the majority of bird field guides, my favorite illustration is a painting by John O'Neill. John's painting of a pair of chachalacas is included in the coffee table-sized book, *John P. O'Neill Great Texas Birds*. The accompanied description was written by John Rowlett. John wrote:

> This plain bird with the poetic name exists somewhere between the Scylla of a chicken and the Charybdis of a curassow. It's a good thing, too, because such asylum has protected most of the dozen or so species of chachalacas from the immoderate hunting pressure visited upon their larger, tastier relatives, the more ornate curassows and guans.

Such a testimony on their taste, however, may not apply for everyone. In Mexico, for instance, they are hunted in many areas of the country. And my naturalist friend George Seaman, while working for the Virgin Islands Wildlife Department, told me that when he attempted to introduce chachalacas to several of the Caribbean islands, the locals "ate them all; they didn't last long."

Harry Oberholser, in *The Bird Life of Texas*, described the plain chachalaca as "A big, rakish, chickenlike bird with a long, dark-green-glossed tail that is broadly tipped with pale brown or whitish. Grayish to olive brown above and on upper breast; light tawny olive on remaining underparts; has pinkish (red in nuptial male) bare skin on each side of chin."

The plain chachalaca is one of the "borderland" birds in the United States; they are found only in the Lower Rio Grande Valley where they utilize forested areas and dense thickets; they are especially common around resacas. They also occur in urban areas with heavy vegetation. They have even adapted to living within many South Texas towns where plantings provide adequate shelter and food.

In *Birding Texas*, Roland Wauer and Mark Elwonger listed chachalacas for Laguna Atascosa and Santa Ana National Wildlife Refuges, Boca Chica Area, Brownsville, Bentsen-Rio Grande Valley and Falcon State Parks, Santa Margarita Ranch, Chapeño, and Salineño.

In Mexico, plain chachalacas occur south of the Lower Rio Grande within the Gulf Coastal Plain to all of the Yucatan Peninsula and to northwest Costa Rica. In *Birder's Mexico*, I wrote about this species at Alta Cima, a tiny Tamaulipan village which I visited on several occasions to participate in Christmas Bird Counts:

During the three days that I camped at Alta Cima, I explored the forested slope above the village along the higher eastern slopes of the Sierra Madre Oriental, as well as the canyons below. Mark [Elwonger] and I left camp first. We wandered through the village, across the upper pasture, and followed the left fork trail into the forest. Almost immediately new sounds greeted us. The first was the mourning whistle-call of the dusky-capped flycatcher. Plain chachalacas, three I think, were next in the upper foliage; these large birds were surprisingly adapted at moving through the canopy with minimal disturbance.

I also wrote about finding plain chachalacas at El Triunfo, a small clearing in the high Sierra Madre de Chiapas, where I was camping with a group of birders:

I also found Prevost's ground-sparrow nearby, a tody motmot and long-tailed manakin on the dry hillside above camp, and an emerald-chinned hummingbird feeding on some red Salvia bushes along the trail. And someone discovered a family of plain chachalacas (until recently considered a separate species and called white-bellied chachalacas) feeding in fruiting trees on the hillside north of camp.

I recall watching the El Triunfo chachalacas as they walked about the tall vegetation. They moved about the upper branches, taking an occasional berry, and seemed more comfortable up high than that did on the ground.

One of the reasons that chachalacas are so widespread in South Texas, is their adaptability to take advantage of feeders that the parks and refuges, as well as local citizens, maintain. These chicken-like birds actually mob the feeders to eat whatever foods are available. I have photographs taken at Sabal Palm and Estero Llano Grande State Park with the feeder platforms crowded with feeding chachalacas. Although these birds are wary in general, they become quite tame wherever they are fed. And the photo blind and the open area at Laguna Atascosa National Wildlife Refuge headquarters almost always offer easy places to photograph chachalacas. The dusty ground also provides dusting sites; chachalacas seem to enjoy dust-bathing.

Oberholser mentioned bird feeders in *The Bird Life of Texas*, thusly:

> The bird alights often in the upper part of a tree and moves to interior branches where it hops and walks about squirrelike as it feeds on berries (hackberries are relished), tender leaves and buds, and a few insects. The chachalaca on occasion eats from the ground but it roosts in trees. Like most gallinaceous birds, it readily eats grain, especially cracked yellow corn. This species and the Green Jay are the chief eaters of corn and bread crumb handouts that are regularly placed in front of the main photographic blind at Santa Ana National Wildlife Refuge, Hidalgo County.

Although chachalacas seem to prefer riparian areas, they get along fairly well in secondary woodlands and thickets. But they have disappeared from areas that have been partially cleared for agriculture and grazing. In the United States they are restricted to riparian, adjacent woodlands, and well wooded urban areas in the southern Valley. They seem to be doing well there, but populations have totally disappeared or have seriously declined within their earlier range to the north.

What the effects of global warming will have on the Texas chachalacas is unsure. So long as riparian habitats remain little changed, they are likely to survive in these native areas. And so long as feeders are maintained, they also will thrive within urban locations in the lower Valley.

Two additional chachalacas occur in Mexico: rufous-bellied chachalaca, West Mexican chachalaca, and white-bellied chachalaca. I recorded the rufous-bellied, sometimes known as West Mexican or Wagler's, chachalaca, in Jalisco. And I found West Mexican chachalacas on the Pacific Slope in southwestern Chiapas.

RED-BILLED PIGEON

This is a large, all-dark bird with a red eye, a red white-tipped bill, and a broad white-tipped square tail. In good light, it shows a purplish back and chest. It is larger than the white-winged dove and the widespread rock dove.

It has a rather distinct call "heard in early spring and summer, a long, high-pitched *cooooo* followed by three loud *up-cup-a-coo* notes," according to Harry Oberholser, in *The Bird Life of Texas*. He also wrote that its call often emanates "from a lofty, often bare branch. Males first emit a mighty upwelling *wooooOOOOOO*, that is followed quickly by usually three *up-cup-a-coo's*. Territory is thus proclaimed from February into August."

Red-bills are a tropical pigeon that barely reach the U.S. in South Texas along the Lower Rio Grande Valley. It apparently was more numerous in earlier years before so much of the Rio Grande floodplain was cleared for agriculture and grazing.

Although U.S. records occur primarily along the Rio Grande from Falcon Dam to near Brownsville, there are several scattered records elsewhere in Texas. Red-bill vagrants have been reported up the Gulf Coast to Corpus Christi and Victoria as well as at Kerrville in the southern edge of the Hill Country.

Timothy Brush wrote about its Valley habitat in *Nesting Birds of the Tropical Frontier*:

> A bird of broken forest in the tropics, the Red-billed Pigeon nests in the tallest, densest riparian forests along the Rio Grande. Most nests I have found have been on forested islands, which are sometimes U.S. territory and sometimes Mexican. These islands are dominated by Mexican ash and sugar hackberry, and I consider the ones most heavily used by Red-billed Pigeons to be high-quality riparian forest.
>
> Red-billed Pigeons may forage in a greater variety of habitats than just tall riparian forest. For example, on September 6, 1999, I saw 18 scattered along the river between Chepéno and Fronton. Some were in possum-grape (*Cissius incisa*) vines laden with fruit; I assumed that they were eating the fruit. A few others were in possum-grape vines in mesquite trees about 1,000 feet (300 m) from the river.

Brush's forested island apparently is one of the most dependable locations to see red-bills in the U.S.; I have seen them there, just above Chepéno, on several occasions. However, it is a difficult bird to find anywhere in the U.S. According to Roland Wauer and Mark Elwonger's *Birding Texas*, records exist only for Bentsen-Rio Grande Valley State Park, Anzalduas County Park, Chepéno, Salinéno, and San Ygnacio.

An historical perspective of red-bills in the U.S. was provided by Oberholser, thusly:

> Breeds, mid-Feb. to mid-Aug. (eggs, Feb. 21 to Aug. 5) from near sea level to about 275 ft. Uncommon and very local (formerly fairly common) in Rio Grande delta, becoming scarce upriver to Falcon Reservoir, and up coast to Norias in Kenedy Co. (nesting north of delta unconfirmed); rare during coldest months.

Later, in 2004, Mark Lockwood and Brush Freeman wrote, in *Handbook of Texas Birds*, that red-bills are "Locally uncommon to rare summer resident in the western Lower Rio Grande Valley. Red-billed Pigeons are found primarily in close association with the Rio Grande. The center of abundance for this species in Texas is Hidalgo and Starr Counties."

In Mexico, red-bills occur in the lowlands on both the Pacific and Atlantic Slopes; their range extends southward into Central America. I am most familiar with it in Tamaulipas, about 100 miles south of the Lower Rio Grande Valley. While working to restore Ridley sea turtles at Rancho Nuevo, I conducted bird counts near the nesting beach. I ran twenty-eight censuses from May 2 to May 10, 1978. I wrote about those surveys in *My Wild Life, A Memoir of Adventure within America's National Parks* as follows:

> Also, during my two-week stay at Rancho Nuevo, I established five transects that I walked one to five times each, recording all of the birds detected, along with notes on whether they were breeding or in migration. The transects were located in five distinct habitats: a littoral zone with both littoral scrub and mangrove habitats; thorn scrub with either dense vegetation or open in places where grazing occurred; thorn forest where larger trees and shrubs were dominant; and riparian habitat, that was more luxuriant and dense due to the continuous presence of ground water.

I recorded 147 bird species within the five habitats: 82 (56%) were nesting and 65 (44%) were migrants. On two censuses in the littoral scrub habitat, 29 species were recorded; 36 species on one census of the mangroves; 66 species on four censuses in thorn forest; 92 species on five censuses in riparian habitat. The thorn forest and riparian habitats supported the highest number of nesting and transient birds: 57 nesting species in the thorn forest and 43 in riparian, and 35 and 47 migrants, respectively.

Only six of the 82 breeding birds were found to nest in all five habitats: red-billed pigeon, groove-billed ani, ladder-backed woodpecker, Couch's kingbird, olive sparrow, and Altamira oriole.

All of my data from those surveys was later prepared for a report that was published in an article, titled "Avian Population Survey of a Tamaulipas Scrub Habitat," in the autumn 1999 issue of *Cotinga*.

In addition to Rancho Nuevo, I wrote about red-billed pigeons at Alta Cima, a tiny village above Gómez Farias, thusly:

Dawn of December 27, 1989 was clear and cold at Alta Cima. Frost had formed overnight on the grass. Birds were evident only by the calls and songs that rang out around the clearing. The loudest and most obvious were those of the spot-breasted wrens; at least four individuals sang from the undergrowth. A blue mockingbird sang briefly. I detected songs of brown-backed solitaires and gray silky-flycatchers further up the hillside, and an Altamira oriole contributed to the morning chorus. Then a flock of twenty-five to thirty red-billed pigeons suddenly flew across the clearing toward the upper village, where I later learned there was a favorite watering hole.

According to Oberholser, "The redbill is a high swift flier. When viewed against the sky, a group of these pigeons resembles a silhouetted parrot flock, as the height, flight speed, and wing flapping are somewhat similar." And Steve Howell and Sophie Webb, in *A Guide to the Birds of Mexico and Northern Central America*, wrote that their "flight mainly direct but slightly sloppy. In display, climbs with exaggerated deep wingbeats. Then glides in descending circles with wings held in strong dihedral."

Oberholser added that "When the present species alights, however, it is not so parrotlike: Redbills commonly land on high bare limbs; Red-crowned and other mostly green Mexican parrots usually perch on crowns of leafy green trees.

The Redbill drinks while standing on sand and gravel bars of tropical rivers, but otherwise it is not seen a great deal on the ground."

Feeding habitats vary from the high foliage in riparian areas to ground-level. Kent Rylander, in *The Behavior of Texas Birds*, wrote that "They consume berries, acorns, and nuts, showing a weakness for mistletoe. Although most birds fed high in the crowns of trees, some individuals have learned (perhaps from watching Mourning Doves and White-winged Doves) to drop down into the stubble fields to take advantage of waste grain."

Oberholser also wrote about the change of status for red-billed pigeons in the U.S.:

The year 1920 marked the beginning of serious habitat destruction in the Rio Grande delta, this bird's sole U.S. nesting ground. By 1945 approximately 90 percent of the species' breeding trees and shrubs had been removed. Then came two blows which virtually extirpated the species as a U.S. bird: First,

the great freeze of 1951 changed the dominant agricultural crop from little-sprayed citrus to cotton which is repeatedly drenched with pesticides and herbicides; and second, the completion in 1953 of Falcon Dam, on the Rio Grande in upper Starr County held back so much water that the water table in the delta dropped drastically, killing all the large native trees.

WHITE-TIPPED DOVE

Almost the size of a mourning dove, the white-tipped dove is plump with whitish underparts, a ruddy-brown back, rufous underwing coverts, and a black, short and rounded tail with white corners; it also has a blue patch in front of each eye that has a yellow iris. Earlier known as white-fronted dove, it is a different genius and species - *Leptotilla verreauxi* - than any of the other members of the family Columbidae.

The white-tip's voice also is unique, a very low-pitched, mournful, three-syllable cooing that often goes unnoticed. The sound has been described as someone blowing across the top of a bottle, and local residents often refer to this dove as "mournful dove." And, unlike its cousins, it almost always sings from concealment.

This dove is one of the "specialty" birds in the United States; it occurs only in the Lower Rio Grande Valley of Texas. However, white-tips possess the largest range of any native Colubid in the New World, extending from South Texas to Argentina.

White-tips are forest and thicket birds; the riparian habitat along the Rio Grande fits their needs perfectly. And they also will utilize dense thicket-like vegetation in urban areas. Mark Elwonger and I, in *Birding Texas*, listed key sites where white-tips can be found in the Valley. We included, east to west, Laguna Atascosa National Wildlife Refuge, Boca Chica, and Brownsville upriver to Resaca De La Palma State Park, Santa Ana National Wildlife Refuge, Bentsen-Rio Grande Valley and Falcon State Parks, and Chapéno and Salinéno. North of the Valley, we listed only Chaparral Wildlife Management Area and Lake Corpus Christi State Park.

Its principal range occurs south of the border in Mexico and southward to Central America. It resides in both the Pacific and Gulf lowlands and throughout the Yucatan, as well as in the southern mountains. Steve Howell and Sophie Webb wrote in *A Guide to the Birds of Mexico and Northern Central America*, that its habitat include a "Wide variety of wooded and forested habitats from brushy thickets to humid evergreen forest (mainly edge) and pine-oak woodland with brushy understory."

The majority of my encounters have been in the Lower Rio Grande Valley, although it is never easily found. I have had the best opportunity by slowly walking toward where it is calling. If startled, it will quickly fly away into the dense vegetation with quick wingbeats. By very slowly advancing toward its call, I have on a couple occasions found it sitting on a limb a few feet above the ground.

In Mexico, it is just as secretive, and getting a good look at one of these doves can be serendipitous. I recall one encounter at El Triunfo in southcentral highlands of Mexico. Although white-tip calls were commonplace around the compound where our group was camped, seeing one was unexpected. I wrote about all the birds found there in *Birder's Mexico*:

> We found small numbers of black-throated jays near our camp and within the forest. I also recorded unicolored jays on the trail toward Finca Prusia. Rufous-browed wrens were fairly common throughout the forest, and although it was heard numerous times, I had only two good observations of this very buffy-colored house-wren. There were three thrushes of special interest at El Triunfo, the mountain and black robins and spotted nightingale-thrush... Additional bird species recorded at El Triunfo included: band-tailed pigeon, white-tipped dove, singing quail, mottled and fulvous owls...

Nests of white-tipped doves are well hidden in tangles of vines or in dense thickets, and Paul Ehrlich and colleagues, in *The Birder's Handbook*, wrote that nests are located

"At fork of inclined branch; flimsy, and usu[ally] of crossed sticks and twigs of grasses." They also are known for keeping their nest and immediate surroundings neat and clean.

Kent Rylander, in *The Behavior of Texas Birds*, discussed white-tip courtship and nesting:

> The male hunches his shoulders, lowers his head, and runs toward the female, only to stop suddenly and coo. Birds also perform a bowing display... Nesting in dense bush or at the fork of an inclined branch. Nest: probably built by both parents, a flimsy structure made from sticks and weed stems. Eggs: presumedly incubated by both parents. Probably both parents feed crop milk to the nestlings.

Although white-tips are "highly terrestrial," they do spend time on the ground where they feed primarily on seeds; and they do take advantage of seed feeders, as well. Harry Oberholser, in *The Bird Life of Texas*, wrote that the white-tip picks most of its food – seeds of hackberry, elm, ebony, anaqua, mesquite, pricklypear cactus, grasses, corn, sorghum, and a few crickets – off the ground or from low branches. It has also been reported taking insects, like butterflies and moths. And like other Columbidae, it requires water and drinks by the usual pigeon method.

White-tips are non-migratory, and ornithologists report that it is more aggressive than any of the doves, often chasing other white-tips from their foraging grounds. Oberholser also wrote about white-tip behavior at Santa Ana, thusly:

> On a primitive road which tunnels through this greenery, one or two of these rather solitary doves can usually be seen all times of the year as they stroll about on their carmine feet. At the slightest alarm, they will scurry or fly into dense cover...Flight is swift in spite of the bird's heavy body and ground-dwelling habit; however, it does not ordinarily fly above the treetops as do White-wing Doves and Red-billed Pigeons.

White-tipped doves seem to be holding their own in undisturbed habitats, such as the riparian and dense thicket areas in the Lower Rio Grande Valley. And in Mexico, in spite of being subject to hunting, they have maintained stable populations in isolated areas. Oberholser wrote:

> Exceptions occur in heavily poisoned stands; for example, in the excessively hydrocarboned (from agricultural dusts and sprays in surrounding cotton and other fields) ebonies along the Olmito Resaca, Cameron County, the Whitefront population died out about 1960. In Texas, the present [1974] dove seems to have a fair chance to survive to the 1980s in the less cleared and poisoned portions of its range especially in Starr and Willacy counties.

So long as the essential Valley habitats are protected, such as at Santa Ana National Wildlife Refuge and Bentsen-Rio Grande Valley State Park, white-tip populations are likely to persist in the United States.

HOOK-BILLED KITE

I have spent considerable time birding the Lower Rio Grande Valley, yet I have encountered hook-billed kites there only a few times. Since it is a tropical species that barely reaches the United States, the two best locations for finding this bird in the U.S. are Bentsen-Rio Grande Valley State Park and Santa Ana National Wildlife Refuge.

My lifer hook-billed kite, however, occurred at Catemaco, Veracruz, in Mexico. I recorded it there on a January 1976 Christmas Bird Count. But my only photograph of this raptor (below) is one I found in Belize. Driving the highway near Dangriga, I discovered a female hook-bill sitting on a snag very near the roadway, and when I stopped for a better look, it stayed. I was able to climb out of my vehicle and get a quick photo before it flew away. Its reddish, barred underside and black tail with two wide, white bands were obvious.

Hook-bills truly are distinguished birds. Adult males are very dark overall, but with a finely-banded, black-and-white chest and legs; females also are dark but their underside is banded rusty-orange. And the head of both sexes is distinct: white eyes, a large, bare, pea-green patch in front of each eye, and a large and heavily hooked, sharp bill. Hook-bills also possess a dark plumage, a dark morph that is overall slate color except for a very wide, white tail band. These birds are exceptional!

And Kent Rylander, in *The Behavior of Texas Birds*, described its flight as "quite distinctive: the longish wings are narrower at the base than toward the tip and have been described as spoonlike or paddle-shaped. The wings are flapped rather loosely and then held fairly flat, often pressed forward and sometimes raised slightly."

I don't recall ever hearing a voice of a hook-bill; they seldom vocalize. But Steve Howell and Sophia Webb, in *A Guide to the Birds of Mexico and Northern Central America*, claim their voice is "a rapid, slightly clipped, chuckling chatter, *weh keh-eh-eh-eh-eh-eh-eh-eh-eh-eh-eh* or *w-keheheheheheheh*." And Harry Oberholser wrote in *The Bird Life of Texas*, that "Hook-billed Kites harassing a Black Hawk were heard to scream and chatter harshly. A musical whistle is also uttered. The Texas birds' apparent alarm note was an almost constant loud rattle call descending in pitch."

Howell and Webb also wrote about their range: hook-bills are "U to F resident on Atlantic Slope from Tamps to Honduras, on Pacific Slope Isthmus to Honduras. R to U on Pacific Slope N of Isthmus to Sin, and inland locally in W cen Mexico to Mex (SNGH, PP); formerly perhaps to DF and Gro. and Gto….from S Texas to N Argentina."

It also occurs, oddly enough, on the Caribbean island of Grenada, but nowhere else in the West Indies. I mentioned this occurrence in *A Birder's West Indies, An Island-by-Island Tour*, thusly: "Grenada has only one single-island endemic, the Grenada dove, but it has several additional species that do not occur elsewhere in the Lesser or Greater Antilles. For instance, the same Hook-billed Kite that occurs from Texas to South America is found on Grenada."

In Mexico, I have recorded hook-billed kites only a few times; I wrote about one of those sightings in *Birder's Mexico*:

> En route back to Valladolid and Highway 180 we found a side road only three miles south of Rio Lagartos, which entered an area of thorn forest that seemed relatively undisturbed. We left our vehicle on the side road and spent a couple hours exploring this habitat. The morning was already very warm, and we found few birds. However, two of those made our stop there worth the effort: hook-billed and double-toothed kites. Both birds were seen from close range. The hook-billed kite had been expected, although I could not help but be impressed with its lumbering flight. But the double-toothed kite seemed out of place; it is more a bird of the heavier forests than of the thorn forest habitat. As we walked back to the car, we "herded" eight black-throated (or Yucatan) bobwhites ahead of us; another of the area's specialties.

Hook-billed kites were first found in the United States in 1964 when a nesting pair was discovered at Santa Ana National Wildlife Refuge. I remember that date very well. I heard about these birds while I was birding near Catemaco in Veracruz. Our group of birders (Ben Basham, Arnold Small, Jim and Cilla Tucker, Betty Wauer, and I) decided to cut our Mexico trip short a day and head back to Santa Ana with the hope of seeing this bird; it would be a new U.S. lifer for all of us. As a result, we drove more than 2,000 miles without an overnight stop, reaching McAllen, Texas late at night. And the very next morning at dawn we were at Santa Ana where we did find our bird.

Timothy Brush provided a good discussion about this tropical species in *Nesting Birds of a Tropical Frontier*, thusly:

> Although not particularly shy, the Hook-billed Kite is nonetheless difficult to find, both in the United States and in the tropical parts of its range. Hook-billed Kites do not forage conspicuously, unlike most raptors... The snails are the main prey items, which must be sought in dense scrub or forest...In Texas I have seen foraging Hook-billed Kites perch on the ground or a short distance above it, taking off only when approached closely. I estimate that I have seen Hook-billed Kites on less than one of fifteen field trips I have made in the Valley. Although perhaps somewhat more readily seen during the nesting season, when it is busy foraging for its offspring, the species is never a sure thing.

Brush also wrote about nesting hook-billed kites at Bentsen-Rio Grande Valley State Park:

> Nesting is conducted in the hot summer months, usually in areas not visited much by birders. A pair with a nest 13-14 feet up along a trail at Bentsen on June 27, 1996, apparently dismantled the nest once I had seen it – it was completely gone when I returned early the next morning. Most nests in the drier northern part of the kite's range in Texas, Tamaulipas, and Nuevo Leon have been found in huisache, less than 25 feet up…Like many tropical hawks, these kites raise only one or two young per nest. Both parents attend the nest, and they have been seen bringing in many snails per hour to their youngsters. The nest itself is like a large dove nest, being constructed of a limited number of sticks, so that the eggs or young can be seen through the bottom of the nest.

Hook-bills are sedentary birds, but they do make short flights over the forest canopy, especially during the early morning hours. Those flights alternate with short glides with wings held flat. They are well adapted for extracting snails from shells with their slender, decurved bills. They also will feed on aquatic creatures such as frogs and insects. Even if hook-bills cannot readily be located, evidence of their presence can usually be found by locating piles of shells on the ground beneath favorite perches.

Oberholser wrote that: "A pile of empty snail shells on the forest floor should prompt an upward investigation, as the Hookbill often drops remains of its preferred food – land and arboreal snails – at the foot of its regular feeding perch and also beneath its nest. The snail eaten in Texas was *Bulimulus alternatus*, a common dryland species."

The long-term survival of hook-bills in the United States is unsure due to climate change. Because their current habitat in South Texas is already at a minimum, increasing temperatures, even slight increases, may have severe detrimental effects on the bird's essential habitat and food. Drying conditions are likely to eliminate the bird's necessary food supply.

WHITE-TAILED HAWK

Adult white-tailed hawks are striking birds! They possess a snow-white tail, with a coal-black subterminal band; immaculate white underparts, although females often possess dark barring on the belly; gray back and head, with dark cheeks; black upper wings and chestnut shoulders (upperwing coverts); and long, two-toned, pointed wings (similar to those of a Swainson's hawk). The wings give it a rather distinct appearance that helps identify it even from a distance. William Clark and Brian Williams, in *A Field Guide to Hawks: North America*, point out that the long, pointed wings "pinch in abruptly to the body on the trailing edge." Juveniles and subadults look very different and have been confused with several other broad-winged hawks.

The white-tail's call has been described as a high-pitched cackling, suggestive of a laughing gull, although to my ear it is less strident and more musical. It is a clear, two-syllable "kee-yah, kee-ha," although excited individuals also utter high-pitched chatter notes. John Tveten in *Birds of Texas*, described its call as a "series of cries, "kil-la kil-la [that] is surprisingly high-pitched and musical for so large and powerful a bird of prey."

The white-tailed hawk, *Buteo albicaudatus* to scientists, is one of Texas's "specialty" birds; its U.S. range occurs only in Texas, although south of the border it extends to Argentina. The Texas birds are full-time residents, residing only on the coastal prairies and adjacent South Texas brushland. They do not migrate, although wandering juveniles can be misconstrued as migrants.

Their range in Texas runs from the Rio Grande Delta northward to a line from Anahuac National Wildlife Refuge in Chambers County to the center of Colorado County and from there to a point several miles above Laredo. Vagrants, however, have been recorded up to 2,000 feet elevation in the Trans-Pecos, north to the Balcones Escarpment, and east into Louisiana.

The white-tail's preferred habitat is the broad coastal grasslands with scattered mesquite and yucca and the occasional oak mottes. They have little competition in this habitat; the only other breeding raptors there include the crested caracara and the occasional red-tailed and Harris' hawks, both of which require heavier woods. In addition, white-tails seem to be very compatible with grazing cattle.

Like other grassland hawks, white-tails nest on low shrubs, such as nonnative Macartney rose clumps, and trees in the open, where they construct bulky, unkempt platform of sticks and twigs that may be refurbished from the previous year or built anew. Nests usually are lined with green twigs, leaves and grass. Nests sometimes are built on old nests of American crows or crested caracaras. Almost all provide a commanding view of the surrounding prairie.

Arthur Cleveland Bent, in his classic *Life History of North American Birds of Prey*, described several representative sites: "any bush rising a little about the surrounding level; an immense nest on the top of a large Spanish bayonet (Yucca), and some twelve feet high and a low record of 15 feet from the ground in a crotch of a large mesquite" and "on a scrub oak, not more than a foot and a half from the ground." Some nests can reach three feet across. The 69 nest dates reported by Bent for Texas ranged from February 1 to July 4.

Reports of courtship displays have been rare. Craig Farquhar watched several times as male birds, perched on the ground near a female, made what seemed to be ritual tugs at clumps of grass. Stick carrying, in which a stem or stick, some over three feet in length and too long to be useful in nest-building, was deposited on a completed nest, was observed on several occasions. And Mark Kopeny, researching in Kleberg County, once observed what he took to be a probably mating display in which a male, before egg-laying commenced, carried a long stick aloft, transferred it from beak to feet, and dropped and retrieved it in mid-air. These instances, together with the talon-grappling flights described by the Palmers below, constitute pretty much the complete record of courtship among white-tailed hawks.

One of the few extensive descriptions of flight displays was provided by Paul and Nancy Palmer (per. com). They documented their observations in Kleberg County thusly:

> Two adult White-tails were vigorously interacting about 100 m from us, at between 10 and 150 m elevation. The higher hawk suddenly drew its wings into an angular configuration and close to the body and dived toward the other. As it approached, the lower bird turned over so that its upperparts faced the ground, presenting outstretched talons. The diving bird spread its wings, slowing its descent; the birds touched talons; the lower bird resumed normal flight posture; and the upper bird regained some of its altitude. Both continued to interact, flying around each other in tight circles and appearing entirely oblivious to the other raptors around them. We watched them very closely, hoping to witness more of what we hypothesized to be courtship flight.

Within four minutes one of the pairs rose to an elevation of 150 m, 50 m above the other, and dived toward the lower bird. The second bird again rolled over and offered its talons. On that pass, the two hawks grasped each other's talons and, with wings and tails loosely spread, made seven complete rotations around a common axis. They did not spin in a simple plane either parallel or perpendicular to the ground surface. Instead they wobbled wildly like a child's top or a toy gyroscope in the final turns. The centrifugal force generated must have been considerable. When they released, they had dropped to 60-75 m. The whirling fall had taken 6-8 seconds. After that dramatic display the two showed little special interest in each other and soon drifted away from our position.

I have seen similar talon-touching of white-tails on a few other occasions, including two sub-adults near Ricardo that tumbled from 65 to 60 m high to ground-level. They may have actually struck the ground while still engaged, but the landing site was concealed by a vine-covered fence. One of the birds flew away from the landing spot within seconds.

When nesting, the female normally lays a clutch of two eggs, dull white to bluish white with brownish markings, but one to three eggs are not unusual. Incubation requires 31 days, with chicks hatching one day apart, according to Farquhar. After 14 days the chicks are alert and begin to utter two vocalizations, a "nee-ow" and a sucking "tsick" note. Nestlings feed themselves at 28 days and normally leave the nest 54 to 57 days after hatching.

White-tailed hawks hunt the open prairie for small mammals, especially cottontails and wood rats, birds, snakes, lizards, frogs, and even insects. Although they occasionally hunt from a perch, more typical hunting behavior is in-flight, either while soaring or hovering 50 to as much as 100 feet above ground level.

Farquhar studied white-tails at the Attwater Prairie Chicken National Wildlife Refuge, where he found that mammals made up about 45 percent of the biomass consumed. Birds made up more than 33 percent, including over 13 percent prairie chickens; reptiles over 16 percent; insects about 5 percent. White-tailed hawks that occur in the Tropics also prey upon small monkeys, such as marmosets.

The bird's hunting behavior also was described by Harry Oberholser in *The Bird Life of Texas*:

> If its keen eye glimpses anything interesting below, the hawk hovers helicopterlike. If either seabreeze or norther be strong, the big raptor is able to remain stationary in the air for some minutes by facing into the wind and hanging spread eagle; in calm weather this bird has to flap considerably

to remain aloft in one spot. When prey definitely reveals itself, the White-tailed Hawk drops. Often the animal slithers or scurries to safety before the bird arrives, in which happenstance the hawk checks its fall and flaps to regain altitude. If the raptor plunges all the way to the grass, it is quite likely, especially in summer, to pin a snake to the ground. After a few minutes, the White-tailed Hawk usually flies away carrying the reptile, either coiled in its talons or dangling in its beak.

Noel and Helen Snyder, in *Birds of Prey: Natural History and Conservation of North American Raptors*, claim that the white-tail's hunting behavior "strongly resembles that of the short-tailed hawk. Both species forage from such high altitudes that they are likely to be overlooked, and both hover in the wind as they patiently inspect the terrain for potential victims."

Another fascinating behavior of white-tails, both adults and juveniles alike, is their attraction to prairie fires, undoubtedly a learned behavior. At prescribed burns at Aransas National Wildlife Refuge, Wayne and Martha McAlister reported that these hawks "not only cruise freshly burned tracts but also actively work the line of flames, swooping down on fleeing cotton rats and grabbing grasshoppers in mid-air to eat on the wing. They usually are seen in ones or twos, but one burn of Aransas attracted 14 and another 28." And, Paul (per. com.) and Nancy Palmer and Sharon Bartels of Kingsville observed a concentration of 56 white-tails at a large (650-8750 ha) prescribed burn on Brooks and Kenedy Counties on March 1, 1987. And Allen Chaney and Tom Urban have on two more occasions seen concentrations of more than 60 white-tails during burns at this same site. On at least one of those occasions, Professor Chaney counted over 100 white-tailed hawks. In each of these instances, more than 75 percent of the birds were in juvenal to sub-adult plumage. Such hunting conditions require only minimal skill.

Brown and Amadon, in *Eagles, Hawks and Falcons of the World,* call this type of raptor behavior "whirling." However, no report of such behavior as part of mating displays occurs for white-tails in any of the literature. The February dates, however, when these displays occurred would be right for mating behavior. There is a previously published report of an instance of inter-specific talon-grappling tangential to an act of "kleptoparasitism" in which a Swainson's hawk was robbed by a white-tailed hawk.

When nesting, the female normally lays a clutch of two eggs, dull white to bluish white with brownish markings, but one or three eggs are not unusual. Incubation requires 31 days, with chicks hatching one day apart, according to Farquhar. After 14 days the chicks are alert and begin to utter two vocalizations, a "nee-ow" and a sucking "tsick" note. Nestlings feed themselves at 28 days and normally leave the nest 54 to 57 days after hatching.

Like so many birds of prey, as well as numerous other birds, raptors were seriously impacted by the use of DDT during the 1960s. White-tailed hawks were not exempt. Populations of many of these birds were documented by Christmas Bird Counts, and that data suggests that white-tail populations since then have made a remarkable recovery. Today's population has apparently more than doubled since an estimate of 200 pairs in 1977. Within their expected range in Texas, white-tails are plentiful and easily found on the coastal prairie.

Some of the easiest places to observe them are along US 87 between Victoria and Raymondville, along State Highway 35 between Port Lavaca and Portland, along State High 185 between Port O'Connor and Seadrift, and at Laguna Atascosa National Wildlife Refuge in Cameron County. The morning hours are best, when the birds are still perched on various posts or are hunting. By mid-day they often are soaring at such heights that they are next to impossible to locate.

GRAY HAWK

The gray hawk is a mid-sized, broad-tailed hawk, smaller than a red-tail but larger than a broad-winged hawk. As suggested by its name, adults are overall gray color except for their black-and-white, broadly banded tail. Another feature of adult gray hawks is their finely banded gray underparts. And in flight, they show rounded wingtips with dark tips. Kent Rylander, in *The Behavior of Texas Birds*, described their flight as "swift, graceful, and agile...appears more like that of a falcon or accipiter than a buteo." Because of their behavior, they were earlier known as "Mexican goshawk." And when perched, they stand more upright than other raptors.

I have often been first attracted to gray hawks by their distinct calls, a loud descending or mournful whistles. Rylander wrote that they possess "A variety of calls, many high, slurred, and flutelike, including a musical piping and a scream (*kree e e*)."

Gray hawks are tropical species that are found in the United States only in southeastern Arizona and in Texas where it occurs in Big Bend National Park, the Davis Mountains, and the Lower Rio Grande Valley. There also are a few scattered records elsewhere in the state.

South of the border, gray hawks can be found along the Pacific and Gulf Slopes southward to northern Argentina. In general, this hawk occurs in the lowlands, and rarely is found above approximately 3500 feet elevation.

Its preferred habitats, according to Steve Howell and Sophie Webb, in *A Guide to The Birds of Mexico and Northern Central America*, include "Wooded and forested habitats, less often semiopen areas with scattered trees. Perches conspicuously on telegraph poles and roadside trees."

My encounters with gray hawks have occurred at several places in the United States and in numerous locations in Mexico. My earliest U.S. observations were in the Lower Rio Grande Valley at Santa Ana National Wildlife Refuge. I had driven to the Valley from Big Bend National Park to see a number of birds that were "special" to that area of Texas. At the time, gray hawks were one of those specialties. I recall seeing my first one while walking along the dike just beyond the visitor center/headquarters area. I was attracted to its descending whistle call, and then it briefly flew into the open. Although I saw it for less than ten seconds, there was no doubt about its identity. Ever since that first time, I have seen it at Santa Ana on numerous occasions.

I also got acquainted with the gray hawk while working at Big Bend National Park (1966-72). My first Big Bend encounter was on April 3, 1970 when I found one soaring low over the Rio Grande at Boquillas Crossing; that sighting represented the first record for the park. It was several years later, during the first half of the 1990s, when it began to nest regularly at Rio Grande Village and Cottonwood Campgrounds.

Gary Clark, in *Book of Texas Birds*, wrote about watching gray hawks at Cottonwood Campground, thusly:

> My wife and I once had the joy of watching parenting behavior by gray hawks at Cottonwood Campground in Big Bend National Park. Both parents were squealing at the youngster in sharply high-pitched whistles while perched about a hundred feet away. Seems they were hell-bent to get the kid to fly. They even showed the young'un how to fly by soaring high in the sky and diving in acrobatic flights like the elite Blue Angels of the U.S. Navy.

Several other bird species have begun nesting in the park during the last thirty years. I wrote about those birds in *For All Seasons, A Big Bend Journal*: "The first Cooper's hawk nests were recorded at Rio Grande Village and Cottonwood Campground in 1992 and 1993. Gray hawks, a bird that was recorded only three times before 1971, have nested at Rio Grande Village annually since 1988."

In addition, I included the following discussion about gray hawks at Big Bend in *A Field Guide to Birds of the Big Bend*:

> Gray Hawk. *Buteo nitidus*. Uncommon summer resident; casual migrant and winter visitor. This bird has nested in the park presumedly only since 1988. Since then it has been found nesting at RGV every year and at CC [Cottonwood Campground] at least in 1989; Willem Maane discovered a "large stick nest" on April 22. Summer records at RGV increased steadily during the 1980s, and Bill Bourbon discovered the first nest, "lined with fresh green leaves," on April 29, 1988. Numerous birders have observed nesting activities there every year since, except possibly in 1986...Sighting elsewhere in the park are few and far between.

Gray hawk records in Texas were later discussed by Mark Lockwood and Brush Freeman in *Handbook of Texas Birds* (2004):

> Rare to locally uncommon resident along the Rio Grande corridor from Hidalgo County to Webb County. Gray Hawks are very rare to casual residents north along the Coastal Prairies to southern Kleberg County. They are rare and summer residents in the Trans-Pecos in Big Bend National Park and very rare in the Davis Mountains. There are out-of-range records from El Paso, Rufugio, and Val Verde Counties.

In Mexico, I have encountered gray hawks on numerous occasions. I recall one early morning at Palenque while birding the hotel grounds and edges. I wrote about that day in *Birder's Mexico*:

> Wandering about the grounds, it would not be unusual to find blue-crowned motmot, both the citreoline and violaceous trogons, two of the large-billed tropical birds, chestnut-collared aracari and keel-billed toucan, yellow-bellied elaenia, royal flycatcher, three euphonias (scrub, yellow-throated and olive-backed), masked tanager, yellow-tailed oriole, and both the chestnut-headed and Montezuma oropendola. Once on the morning of Christmas Eve, from a perch atop the Temple of Inscriptions, I recorded six outstanding raptors. The double-toothed kite and bicolored hawk were seen along the edge of the forest. Gray, short-tailed and white hawks and bat falcon were observed flying directly over the ruins.

I wrote about another gray hawk encounter at Quiahuiztlan, an archeological site in Veracruz, in *Ruins to Ruins*:

> My first impression of Quiahuiztlan was that it was dominated by a tall, massive basalt plug with sheer cliffs on three sides. The huge structure, known as "Penon de Bernal," had a trail to the summit. Later, after walking about the ruins, we climbed to the top where we were enchanted by the incredible panorama...There was little vegetation directly around the ruins,

but we could see mature forest in all directions except for the coastline, which was fringed with greenery. We found two birds of interest on our climb. We saw a gray hawk while climbing the steep slope; it was sitting on top of a small tree off to the right, and it allowed us an excellent view through our binoculars. When we reached the summit, a pair of red-billed pigeons flew out from the trees below; we must have walked right by them earlier.

The status of the gray hawk in Mexico is fairly stable, although the massive land-clearing activities in many parts of the country for agriculture and grazing will certainly have major consequences. In the United States, the few habitats which currently support breeding gray hawks are in danger primarily due to the loss of habitat from droughts due to global warming. The exceptions may be localities that are artificially maintained, such as campgrounds at Big Bend National Park and elsewhere.

APLOMADO FALCON

The aplomado falcon, known to scientists as *Falco fermoralis* is only about three- quarter the size of its larger, more powerful cousin, the peregrine, but it is almost twice the size of the smallest U.S. falcon, the American kestrel. Each of these raptors kill their prey by biting them with their unique tomial tooth, the cutting edge of the upper bill and the corresponding notches on the lower bill. Only falcons possess a tomial tooth. The name aplomado is derived from the Spanish word "leadened," referring to the gray color of the bird's back.

Tom Cade, in *Falcons of the World*, provided an additional description of falcons:

> They have typical raptorial feet with a hallux acting in opposition to three forward toes, all with a powerful grasping ability and armed with sharp, curved talons; they have hooked bills with a strong bite; fleshy ceres at the base of the upper beak; and remarkable powers of vision with lateral and binocular foveae in the retina of each eye.

Aplomado falcons differ little from other falcons. They possess long wings and tail that is finely banded, a gray-black back and cap, a broad white eyeline, and a distinct black moustachial stripe. The front of an adult aplomado, however, is unique. Its chest is snow white, it possesses a broad, blackish chest-band, and a cinnamon belly and thighs. At rest, its black-and-white, banded tail extends beyond the wingtips. It is a remarkable bird!

The voice of the aplomado falcon was described by Steve Howell and Sophie Webb, in *A Guide to the Birds of Mexico and Northern Central America*, as "A full screaming *keeh-keeh-keeh*…and a single sharp *keeh* or *kiih*."

There are several excellent illustrations of aplomados in bird books and elsewhere. The painting by R. David Digby of an adult and an immature male in Tom Cade's book is exceptional. But, my favorite aplomado painting is one by John O'Neill; print number 18 hangs in my office. John's painting was part of an early effort to attract birders to join the American Birding Association (ABA); all lifetime members received a print. ABA, started by Jim Tucker with 12 members in 1969, had, by 2007, grown to more than 12,000 members in 100 foreign countries.

The aplomado falcon is largely a tropical species which occurs all along the Gulf Coastal Plain as far north as Texas. It also occurs irregularly in the Chihuahuan Desert of Mexico, southern New Mexico, and West Texas. During the six years that I lived at Big Bend National Park, I checked out more than a dozen reported aplomado reports, but none of those reports were verified. It was not until I was birding at Palenque, Veracruz, that I finally succeeded in seeing one of these birds. While birding behind the Palenque ruins, I and my companions – Jim and Cilla Tucker, Arnold Small, Benton Basham, and my wife Betty - encountered a couple birders who mentioned seeing an aplomado falcon in downtown Palenque. I wrote about that sighting in *Birder's Mexico*:

We learned that the bird waited until late dusk, just when the village street lights were turned on, to fly down one side of the street, make a loop around the lighted square, and go back down the opposite side of the street and away. Apparently, it found easy meals of numerous cicadas around the lights at that time of evening. We arrived at the plaza in plenty of time, and situated ourselves on the stone steps of the huge church.

Watching the street in front of us, almost like magic, the minute the lights went on we saw the falcon. I must admit that I had first doubted the whole story, but we watched the bird fly toward us along one side of the street, capturing and eating several insects on the wing. When it circled the plaza, it passed almost directly overhead. Then it headed back down the street and disappeared in the darkening sky. It was one of the easiest lifers I can remember, but I decided to count it anyway.

My next aplomado sighting was in South Texas. A restoration program on the Laguna Atascosa Wildlife Refuge in 1993 had successfully produced a few birds that wandered up the coast to Aransas National Wildlife Refuge. One day while driving to the refuge, I suddenly spotted a thin raptor perched on a roadside utility pole. I stopped, turned around, and drove back to where I could get a better look. It sat there, seemingly undisturbed, while I studied that bird through binoculars for several minutes before it finally flew away.

Like other falcons, aplomados do not build their own nests. They instead appropriate vacant nests of other birds, such as those of caracaras, Harris's hawks, and Chihuahuan ravens. These are loosely constructed platforms of sticks, and are lined with a few grasses. Cade wrote that

> Aplomado falcons use the old stick nests of other birds as their eyries, occasionally also bromeliads. In the Chihuahuan Desert region of Texas, New Mexico and northern Mexico, the falcons usually choose old nests of the white-necked [Chihuahuan] raven located at heights of 8 to 25 feet in yuccas or mesquites, or sometimes those of Swainson's hawks.

And Helen and Noel Snyder, in *Birds of Prey Natural History and Conservation of North American Raptors*, wrote about an aplomado nest they investigated in Veracruz, thusly:

> They were mainly former nests of the Black-shouldered Kites and Roadside Hawks and were located in small groves of trees surrounded by largely open country. Around the nests, the aplomados were not exceptionally wary birds. And at one nest that we climbed to examine the nestlings, we found the female to be highly aggressive, cackling furiously and swooping in with reckless strafing runs, striking us repeatedly with her talons. Roughly the size and weight of a female Cooper's Hawk, she packed considerable power in her blows, and we kept our nest checks very brief to minimize the chances of injury, both to her and to us.

Aplomados are migratory at the northern and southern edge of their range and at high altitudes. Chihuahuan Desert birds, except when droughts limit their food supply, usually remain on their breeding ground year-round. However, that feeding range is likely to expand when prey is limited.

These falcons are long, sleek birds that utilize a chase and grab style to capture prey, mostly birds and insects, although lizards are also utilized. They often fly at dusk, catching insects which they eat in flight. My report above about an aplomado feeding on insects at dusk at Palenque is one example. They also have been reported at prairie fires where they fly along the edge to capture insects escaping the flames.

Cade described their general behavior thusly:

> The aplomado falcon has often been characterized as a rather sluggish bird, more prone to capturing easily taken prey such as grasshoppers, lizards and mice, rather than an active pursuer of birds. This false impression may come from the fact that like many hot climate birds aplomado falcons are not very active in the middle of the day, when they are more likely to be quietly perched on a telegraph pole, fence post or dead tree, occasionally taking a snack of an easily caught insect.

Cade also compared the aplomado's hunting prowess with that of the sharp-shinned hawk in its "stealthy manner of hunting for its prey in thick foliage of the woods, flying near the ground, or perching in secluded places, from whence it watches, cat-like, for quail, ground doves, etc." He added:

> Its most usual method of attacking birds is direct pursuit and tail-chasing. When doves and other birds tried to escape by seeking cover in dense trees or bushes, the aplomado falcon would plunge right into the foliage and often catch the bird off its perch before it could fly out, again revealing its accipiter-like traits; or the female would flush the bird out, and the male waiting in the air above would strike it in the open.

The Snyders wrote that the "virtual disappearance of the aplomado from the United States may have resulted from the over-enthusiastic activities of early egg collectors. But it is a reasonable surmise that habitat degradation and, more recently, DDE and dieldrin contamination have played more important roles."

Aplomados have attracted the attention of conservationists for many years, and during the last half-century, several restoration projects have been initiated. Since 1977, the Peregrine Fund, in collaboration with the U.S. Fish and Wildlife Service, have worked to restore a viable aplomado population to the Chihuahuan grasslands. Since 1993, that program has produced 923 fledglings; 812 were released in South Texas. Of those, 37 pairs were found breeding in the wild, producing 87 wild young.

WHISKERED SCREECH-OWL

Of the three North American screech-owls, only the whiskered screech-owl is truly a tropical species. Its principal range is in Mexico and Central America, and only the northern tip occurs in the U.S. in southeastern Arizona. South of the border, its range extends along the Sierra Madre Occidental to the Isthmus of Techuantepec and south to Belize and Nicaragua.

Less than eight inches tall, it is the shortest of the three screech-owls. But its appearance is similar in that it is overall gray with black streaks on the breast and with short ear-tufts. And red morphs have been reported from central Mexico. A key identifying feature, besides where it occurs, is its rather unique voice. Julio De La Torre, in *Owls Their Life and Behavior*, described its voice as follows:

> Territorial call-series of 4-6 short, mellow, "hooty" whistles on one pitch, delivered at even rhythm about as fast as one can count them, not unlike sound produced by blowing across an open bottle; often transcribed as *boot-boot-boot-boot*. Similar call of screech speeds up; whiskered stays even, may slow down at end. Mating song, often delivered in duet form, strikingly like Morse code - a series of irregularly accented single and double notes, often in short groups of three, a pause, then a fourth, longer terminal note; many other patterns. Alarm notes many are varied.

And Paul Johnsgard, in *North American Owls, Biology and Natural History*, described its voice somewhat differently:

> The typical song consists of 4-8 notes, and is the most prevalent vocalization during territory establishment and pair formation, but declines during the period of copulation and egg laying. The syncopated song was heard when the birds were excited, usually sexually, as when a male presents food to a female, prior to copulation, and during copulation. The song did not appear to be important in territory defense, and more probably serves a role in individual recognition.

My first encounter with this owl was years ago when Bruce Moorhead and I spent June 8 and 9, 1964, birding Arizona's Santa Rita Mountains. The afternoon and evening of June 8 found us wandering along Madera Canyon, and it was a couple hours after dark before we heard a whiskered screech-owl. By walking slowly toward the sound, we arrived beneath an oak tree where the bird was calling. It then took a considerable amount of time, and imitating the bird's song, before we located the owl almost directly above our heads, about a dozen feet away. It seemed unafraid and remained in place looking directly at us for a good two or three minutes before it flew up-canyon and out of view. Although the bird looked very much like the western screech-owl we had seen earlier, we identified it as a whiskered screech-owl primarily due to its Morse-code-like song.

My next encounter with a whiskered screech-owl was in April 1977, when Dick Russell and found one near Jalisco, Mexico. That habitat was a dry riparian area, very different than where I had first recorded one in Arizona.

Whiskered screech-owls are nonmigratory and their habitat preference includes dense oak groves, a sycamore riparian environment with streamside thickets, and an oak-pine association at somewhat higher elevations. In Mexico, according to Steve Howell and Sophie Webb, in *A Guide to the Birds of Mexico and Northern* Central *America*, its habitat is listed as "Oak and pine-oaks forest. Habits much as Eastern Screech-Owl."

Johnsgard added information about the "movement" of whiskered screech-owls, thusly:

> So far as it known, this species is entirely sedentary, and it probably occurs too far south to be significantly affected by winter reductions in insect populations. The northern limit of the species' range occurs at the terminus of the dense, continuous oak woodlands in southern Arizona. It is possible

that some vertical migration to lower elevations occurs during winter, at least at the northern end of the range.

Nesting birds utilize natural cavities or abandoned flicker holes in oaks and sycamores. During courtship, pairs participate in mutual preening, billing, and syncopated duetting. Three to four eggs are laid in late April to early May; females undertake incubation and fledglings are active by early to mid-June.

De La Torre also mentions an unusual behavior of whiskered screech-owls:

> Whereas screech and flammulated owls respond to territorial challenges mostly in the trees they live in, whiskered owls have several times been observed to do battle – or in any case *offer* to do battle - on the ground. This has been the experience of birders who have induced territorial defense by playing tape recordings of whiskered owl songs while standing in moderately large clearings. Perhaps the experience lies in the owl's exceedingly keen hearing, which leads it directly to the source of the sound – the tape recorder, often held at waist level. Whiskered owls will also sometimes waddle up to a man whistling an imitation of their song; Joe Marshall tells of feisty males strutting close enough to be picked up. And they have been known to land on a picnic table and march resolutely toward a cassette player, clearly believing that a rival was hiding inside!

The diet of whiskered screech-owls is varied but they seem to have a preference for moths, a staple item at nesting time. They also prey on beetles in flight, as well as caterpillars, grasshoppers, crickets, spiders, and scorpions caught on leaves, branches and on the ground. And they also take a few small mammals when the opportunity arises. They hunt by making short flights from a perch or on the ground, and catching prey by their talons.

FERRUGINOUS PYGMY-OWL

This little owl was one of my most wanted birds in the United States. Although I had seen it numerous times in Mexico, until I found one in Texas, it remained a high priority bird. That opportunity occurred when I was invited by Paul Palmer to help locate one of these owls on the King Ranch. The managers of the almost one-million-acre King Ranch became interested in ecotourism and asked Paul, who was living in nearby Kingsville, to assess the area's bird life. It was then that Paul, Mike Turner and I made our first visit to this huge semi-wild area in search of that illusive owl.

We began our survey on the Norias division of the King Ranch, the southwestern quarter of the ranch, on November 2, 1989, and we found one individual that very first day. We had stopped along the roadway in a habitat we assumed was the most likely to possess resident pygmy-owls. We climbed out of the vehicle and stood there for several minutes hoping to hear a pygmy-owl. Finally, without hearing our bird, we began imitating its rather distinct call. And almost immediately we got a response. A ferruginous pygmy-owl was responding about fifty to sixty feet away among the mesquites. Mike immediately reacting by jumping up and down in a happy, but half-crazy expressive way; Paul and I could only smile and look at each other.

Although we did not see the vocalist that first day, we soon realized that to find pygmy-owls on the Norias it simply was a matter of driving the various roads and stopping to listen for their easily recognized calls. Their calls are a repetitious, harsh and inflected "poip" notes, often 10 to 60 consecutively, and followed by a 10-second lull before being repeated. I later discovered that male call notes alternate between the "poip" notes and clear whistles. Female calls are higher and more aspirate. Its vocalizations have also been described as a mellow series of "whah" notes, similar to the sound made by blowing across the opening of a partially filled bottle of water.

Unlike most owls, this species is neither strictly nocturnal nor diurnal, but seems to be active at all times of the day or night. Although they call mostly at dawn and dusk, they can often be heard throughout the night and during all the daylight hours as well. But it is most vocal during its nesting cycle that generally extends from April into early June.

The ferruginous pygmy-owl, next to the elf owl, is the smallest North American owl, measuring less than seven inches in length and with a wingspan of about 14 inches. Males weigh in at about 2.2 ounces; females are slightly larger at about 2.6 ounces. These little owls are an overall gray-brown to ferruginous (reddish-brown) color, hence its name. And it lacks any evidence of ear tufts. A frontal view reveals white underparts with ferruginous streaks, a long tail with brown to blackish bars, yellow eyes with black pupils in a gray-brown face, and with eyebrows bordered with whitish lines. And its ferruginous back contains whitish wing and tail bars and a pair of black, oblong eyespots on the nape. These eyespots serve as an extra set of "eyes" that is said to "fool" potential predators.

And the flight of this little owl can be described as "shrike-like," direct and with little undulations. Short flights are commonplace, often with a pause at a perch between each. When perched, it often jerks its tail up and down.

The ferruginous pygmy-owl is generally considered to be a tropical species, found throughout Mexico and as far south as Argentina. Although it was earlier considered only a rare visitor to Texas, it has been known to occur in the state since May 3, 1890, when Major Charles E. Bendire collected a set of eggs near Brownsville. After that first record, it seems to have eluded birders for almost 100 years. Then, from 1972 to 1993, sightings began to be reported regularly in the vicinity of the Rio Grande below Falcon Dam, with a maximum of ten pairs. The "clothes line pole" site at the Boy Scout Camp became famous by the abundant birders that took advantage of a known location where one was likely to find this little tropical owl. I was one of those birders that found it there in 1972.

In 1968, Bruce Fall had reported a "small population" of pygmy-owls on the King Ranch, and on April 4, 1974, Andy O'Neil discovered one at a roadside oak motte "just north of Norias." And in 1975, 1976 and 1983, John Arvin, Peter Reisz (per. com.) and J. R. Bloomberg, respectively, found loners along U.S. 77 between Raymondville and Armstrong.

All of the pre-1989 records might have been attributed to stray birds from Nuevo Leon and Tamaulipas, Mexico. The nearest known Mexico populations occurred near Cerralvo, Nuevo Leon, about 45 miles west of Falcon Dam. And there also was a known population along the Rio Corona and in the Sierra Picacho areas, approximately 140 and 85 miles, respectively, south of the border. Yet none of these populations, due to their small size and distance from the Lower Rio Grande Valley, appeared to provide an adequate recruitment base.

Our November 2, 1989 finding on the King Ranch in a sense opened the door to the discovery of a major population within the United States. Following that initial visit, I worked out arrangements with the King Ranch to establish a series of surveys on the Norias to obtain a better understanding of the pygmy-owl's status. And within the next several months I located an amazing number of individuals. I utilized both driving and walking transects all during 1990 and 1991, and once I was able to identify essential habitats, I also flew the area with pilot Anse Windham on January 3, 1991. That allowed me to better develop percentages of the various habitats within the study area.

I understood the pygmy-owls' preferred habitats consisted of mature mixed live oak-mesquite, live oak mottes, mesquite savannah, and fencerows. And based upon my surveys and aerial observations, along with territorial sizes, I calculated a grand total population as 654 pairs within the two optimum habitats in Kenedy, Brooks and Willacy counties. That population did not include additional pairs within the mesquite savannah and along fencerows. I also came to believe that this extensive Texas population, not the Mexico population, was the recruitment base for the majority of birds found elsewhere in Texas. I then estimated territorial sizes as 8.3 acres in mixed live oak-mesquite, 102.4 acres in live oak mottes, and 410 acres in mesquite savannah.

The huge South Texas population extends southeast to northwest within an area roughly oblong in shape, approximately 85 miles long by 35 miles wide, and encompasses about 1800 square miles. The area extends from six miles west of Port Mansfield (along SH 186) north and northwest to Sarita and Falfurrias.

I then prepared an article, with Palmer and Windham as co-authors, on our entire process, including pygmy-owl population size estimates, that was published in *American Birds* in 1997.

In additional to surveying for ferruginous pygmy-owls during the two years of study on the Norias, I also documented all the birds found during my surveys. I discovered that the Norias contained several birds considered to be South Texas specialties. Those included white-tipped dove, common pauraque, buff-bellied hummingbird, northern beardless-tyrannulet, green jay, long-billed thrasher, tropical parula, olive sparrow, and Audubon's oriole, all considered full-time residents. I was greatly impressed with the wildlife diversity on the Norias; I found that it contained one of the highest biodiversity than anywhere I had worked over my many decades spent in the field.

Since those early years, birders have been able to find pygmy-owls at several of the private ranches within the region, and the King, Kenedy, and El Canelo ranches have been offering birding tours where these owls and the other specialties can be found.

This little owl is non-migratory, and usually is present on its territory year-round. How much movement there may be by fledglings and post-nesting adults is unknown, although it is likely that some individuals do venture away from their breeding grounds. It is these individuals that may account for those birds found along the Rio Grande or along US 77.

The breeding cycle for ferruginous pygmy-owls starts in February or March when males begin to defend select territories. These individuals spend a good part of their night and day singing along the edge of their territory. Although birds may roost on tree limbs, usually reasonably close to the trunks, they are cavity nesters that utilize a wide variety of natural cavities, including abandoned woodpecker nests, as well as artificial nest boxes. Because the golden-fronted woodpecker is common throughout the pygmy-owl's

Texas range, they readily take advantage of that bird's abandoned nests, whether on trees or poles. Live oaks and large mesquites are most often utilized. Nest-holes are often reasonably low to the ground but may be as much as 40 feet high.

Three to four, occasionally two to five eggs, are placed in the bottom of the cavity, often without any nesting material or limited to a few leaves. Gordon Alcorn claimed that ferruginous pygmy-owl eggs are "coarsely granulated" and "much thicker and not smooth" than eggs of other pygmy-owls. Incubation lasts about 30 days, and fledgling normally occurs 28 days after the first egg is hatched. Males feed the female during that period. Although some fledglings immediately leave their nest sites, others may return to the nest to sleep.

The diet of a ferruginous pygmy-owl contains an amazing assortment of creatures, primarily because it can be active during both the daytime and nighttime. Invertebrates, including a huge variety of large insects, spiders, scorpions, and even earthworms may dominate its daily input. But lizards, snakes, frogs, and even small mammals and birds are also taken whenever the opportunity arises. Julio De Torres wrote, in *Owls Their Life and Behavior,* that "it will take on mammals twice its size and pounce on birds as big as thrashers. Fast and nimble on the wing, it goes after and actually catches hummingbirds."

Harry Oberholser, in his monumental book, *Bird Life of Texas*, summarized all pre-1972 ferruginous pygmy-owl records in Texas, and considered it "present in fairly good numbers between 1920 and 1945," but "rare" following the clearing of "90 percent of the mesquite-ebony woodlands of the Rio Grande delta. However, it appears that there has been little decline in the live oak habitats. In fact, there have been documented increases in live oak habitat in the last 100 years."

Because of the additional known populations in recent years, the South Texas populations of this little owl, at least on the King and Kenedy Ranches, appear to be stable. These birds have become important components of the recent ecotourism wave throughout the region.

So long as the various ranches continue their ecotourism practices and refrain from grand scale clearing for additional pastures or other "improvements," the Texas population of ferruginous pygmy-owls is likely to remain intact.

ELF OWL

The elf owl is the world's smallest owl; it is smaller even than the widespread house sparrow. It has a rounded head, no ear tufts, pale reddish facial disks, white "eyebrows," brilliant yellow eyes, and a stubby tail. Its plumage is mottled browns and blacks with an irregular white collar across the hindneck.

The call of an elf owl is an irregular series of high whimpering "churp" notes and chattering. Kent Rylander, in *The Behavior of Texas Birds*, wrote that its voice is "Extraordinarily loud, considering that this is the smallest owl in the world. Call: an excited *whi whi whi whi whi whi whi whi*, as well as yips and barks that suggest a puppy. Complex vocalizations represent a pair calling in duet."

Julio De La Torre, in *Owls Their Life and Behavior*, provided another description of its calls:

> Remarkably varied; J. D. Ligon has described at least a dozen calls. Most often heard is rapid high-pitched series of 6 or more yips or cackling chirps-whi-whi-whi-whi-whi-whi, chewk-chewk-chewk, or tyew-tyew-tyew-tyew, typically rising in pitch and becoming more chattering, yippy, and puppylike in the middle; sung as duet by male and female. Given at night, call is best cue to presence of bird.

The elf owl apparently was a favorite of bird artist John O'Neill, who painted this tiny bird sitting on a mesquite branch with a nest box in the background. John's marvelous painting appears in his coffee table sized book, *John P. O'Neill Great Texas Birds*. Pauline James wrote an accompanying narrative:

> Birding in the Valley has always been exciting, primarily because of the tantalizing idea that almost anything is possible. In recent years more and more avid birders have come to scour the backroads and few remaining stands of brushland, hoping to get lucky and stumble across yet another great new bird for themselves and for South Texas.

The elf owl (*Micrathene whitneyi*) is a bird of the American Southwest and northwestern Mexico. Its range includes all of the southern half of Arizona and all of Sonora, and it extends eastward to Chihuahua, Coahuila, and Tamaulipas in Mexico and the Big Bend Country in Texas. It is a bird of the deserts, utilizing saguaro stands, riparian areas along streams, and oak and pine-oak woodlands from near sea-level to 5,000 feet elevation. It rarely occurs to 7,000 feet.

I am most familiar with the elf owl from my experiences in Big Bend National Park, Texas. In *A Field Guide to Birds of the Big Bend*, I wrote the following about the elf owl:

Fairly common spring migrant and summer resident. Park records extend from one at RGV [Rio Grande Village] on February 24, 1994 to one at PJ [Panther Junction] on October 11, 1985. This tiny owl is most obvious from early March to late April, when they are calling from "posts" along the edge of their breeding territories. By mid- to late April, however, when their territories have been defined and nesting has begun, they become silent and more difficult to find. Three or four pairs nest in the RGV area; they usually nest at Dugout Wells; and several pairs nest along the Window Trail and near the Chisos Basin Amphitheater. I found family groups of adults and three youngsters on two occasions at Dugout: on July 4, 1968, and August 17, 1968. By late June, Elf Owls sometimes can be found at night hunting moths around the lights at RGV and the Chisos Basin.

The elf owl also spends its breeding season in southern Arizona, and elsewhere within the Sonoran Desert. There it takes advantage of cavities constructed in saguaros by gilded flickers and Gila and ladder-backed woodpeckers. The builders use the cavity for only one year, pecking out a new one annually. The construction, however, is normally done in summer or fall, after the nesting season. For the saguaros, the post-nesting construction of new cavities allows the cactus to form a callus over the soft tissue inside the cavity by the following season. The cavity nesters, therefore, rarely utilize nest lining. Elf owls find that the vacant saguaro cavities provide exactly what is required for the breeding season.

In Mexico, elf owls are a common to fairly common local breeder from March to August. Steve Howell and Sophie Webb provided additional details on their Mexican distribution in *A Guide to the Birds of Mexico and Northern Central America*; they report it "on Pacific Slope from Son to N Sin, in interior from Chih to NL, possibly elsewhere S over the Plateau; disjointly in upper Balsas drainage in S Pue. Migrates late Feb-early Apr. Aug-Sep; winters (Sep-Mar) mainly in Balsas drainage from Mich to Pue."

I included a discussion of elf owl life history at Big Bend National Park in *For All Seasons, A Big Bend Journal*, thusly:

March 23 (1968). I heard the first elf owls of the year at the Graham Ranch (at the west end of Rio Grande Village) during an evening visit there. Their strange warble – eight to ten low whistles, like "hew-ew, hew-ew, hew-ew, hew-ew, hew-ew, hew-ew, hew-ew, hew-ew" – was a welcome reminder that the new nesting season had begun. In spring and summer, these tiny owls can be surprisingly common throughout the lowlands and up into the lower edge of the pinyon-juniper woodlands. They are especially evident when they first return from their Mexican wintering grounds. Although many of the adults undoubtedly wander about a good deal in search of suitable nesting sites, nest cavities can include a wide range of places, such as natural cavities or deserted woodpecker nests in utility poles, fence posts, and numerous trees and shrubs. Once a suitable territory is located, the male will spend most of his time calling from singing perches along the edges. But once a female is attracted and mating occurs, birds are far less vociferous and more difficult to locate.

This tiny predator seems to be doing well throughout its range. Except for birders and other nature lovers, however, it is largely unknown. Its nesting habitats are rarely threatened, primarily because of its isolated breeding grounds. However, the removal of nesting sites, such as utility poles or clearing of mesquite or other woody vegetation, or indiscriminate use of pesticides that reduces prey species, are possible. In cases when threats become known, enhancement projects have been established. Pauline James, writing in *John P. O'Neill's Great Texas Birds*, described one project:

> We put up the first houses, on eight-foot fence posts with metal trash can predator guards, and laughed at the idea that any Elf Owl would be interested in making its home there. Two weeks later when we walked up to the post and tapped it, an angry little owl face emerged from the hole! Success!

GROOVE-BILLED ANI

What a strange bird is the groove-billed ani! It is all-black with a long floppy tail, and its bill is large and grooved above and shorter and straight below. The dark eyes seem sunken slightly and are surrounded by pale skin. And in sunlight its back shows iridescent purple and green overtones. And if that isn't enough, its call is a series of squealing notes. Kent Rylander, in *The Behavior of Texas Birds*, described its call as "a rapid, flickerlike PLEE koh PLEE koh PLEE koh PLEE koh; in flight, a variety of clucking sounds. They also produce numerous other sounds (chucks, quacks, whines, etc.), each apparently with its own function."

The bird's grooved bill truly is unique. Gary Clark, in *Book of Texas Birds*, stated that it "looks like a cross between a puffin beak and a parrot beak that's painted black. The upper mandible is eminently arched with bold grooves etched lengthwise across the surface."

The flight of the groove-billed ani also is distinct. In *The Bird Life of Texas*, Harry Oberholser wrote:

> This and the high-arched bill are the chief field marks separating it from the Great-tailed Grackle, which bird it seems to mimic in appearance. The ani jumps into the air from a thorny bush, gives a few quick flaps, then sails for two feet or more, gives another burst of quick flaps, then sails, etc. Upon arriving at the next bush, the bird lands, at which time the long, loose tail flops forward over the bird's back – sometimes almost toppling said ani off its perch.

Timothy Brush added a comment on its behavior in *Nesting Birds of a Tropical Frontier*, thusly:

> A flock of anis is amusing to watch as they fly and hop erratically around a shrub or tree. The large bill is used to capture large insects, such as grasshoppers, which the birds often pursue down to the ground. At least during fall migration, anis readily consume small fruits such as granjeno and seeds like *Urvillae*. The species is an occasional nest predator, and I have seen other bird species pursue and harass anis in open fields in Belize. Valley birds do not seem to recognize anis as predators, so perhaps that habit is limited to tropical areas.

The groove-billed ani is a tropical bird that reaches the United States only in South Texas, particularly in the lowlands along the Rio Grande from the Big Bend Country in the west to the Gulf Slope on the east. It also occurs irregularly along the Gulf Coast to Florida. In Mexico, it is "resident on both slopes from S Son and N Coah to El Salvador and Honduras," according to Steve Howell and Sophie Webb in *A Guide to the Birds of Mexico and Northern Central America*.

Most of my ani encounters are from the years that I worked at Big Bend National Park. In *A Field Guide to Birds of the Big Bend*, I wrote the following:

> Groove-billed Ani. *Crotophaga sulcirostris*. Sporadic summer visitor and migrant. The first record for the Trans-Pecos was one collected north of the park at the Black Gap WMA [Wildlife Management Area] by W. Frank Blair in June 1961. And on May 21, 1968, one of two birds seen at Rio Grande Village was collected (Wauer 1968).
> The RGV birds represented only the second authenticated record of the species for the Trans-Pecos. Since these first records, the Groove-billed Ani has been reported sporadically in late spring and summer at RGV and the adjacent floodplain, arriving in June and remaining until October.

I also wrote about my initial ani sightings in *For All Seasons, A Big Bend Journal*:

July 26 (1969). I discovered a pair of groove-billed anis constructing a huge nest at Rio Grande Village today. The nest was located about fifteen feet high in a cottonwood along the nature trail. Both adults shared in the nest-building activities, carrying billfuls of twigs, dead leaves, and grasses to the growing structure. That nest was never utilized, however; it was deserted in a day or two. But on August 5, I found two anis, presumedly the same birds, building two separate nests in a cottonwood at the northwest corner of the campground. They deserted these nests as well.

Since then, vagrant groove-billed anis have been recorded throughout the state in summer, and there also are a few isolated nesting records as far north as Tom Green and Lubbock Counties, according to Mark Lockwood and Brush Freeman, in the *Handbook of Texas Birds*. The vast majority of anis move south during the winter months.

In Mexico, I found groove-bills common in avian surveys I conducted at Rancho Nuevo in Tamaulipas. I wrote about those avian surveys in *Birder's Mexico*, thusly:

During a two-week stay I established five transects that I walked one to five times each, recording all of the birds detected. The transects were located in five distinct habitats: a littoral zone with both littoral scrub and mangrove habitats; thorn scrub with either dense vegetation or open in places where grazing occurred; thorn forest where larger trees and shrubs were dominant; and riparian habitat that was more luxuriant and denser due to the continuous presence of ground water.

I recorded 147 bird species within the five habitats: 82 (56%) were nesting and 65 (44%) were migrants…Only 6 of the 82 breeding birds were found to nest in all five habitats: red-billed pigeon, groove-billed ani, ladder-backed woodpecker, Couch's kingbird, olive sparrow, and Altamira oriole.

Since the initial records at Big Bend, groove-bill sightings have been few and far between. For the Trans-Pecos in general, Jim Peterson and Barry Zimmer wrote, in *Birds of the Trans-Pecos* (1998), that it is "Fairly common resident in spring and summer around

Del Rio area (Val Verde County). Rare visitor in spring and summer in Big Bend country; Casual at all seasons north of the Big Bend. With only two records from the El Paso area."

Unlike other members of the Cuckoo Family (Cuculidae), that Includes roadrunners and cuckoos, anis engage in cooperative breeding. Rylander wrote:

> It nests in a low tree or shrub, one to four pairs build together a bulky structure of sticks and other plant materials, in which all the females in the group deposit their eggs. Additionally, all parents incubate the eggs (normally, the dominant male at night) and all care for the nestlings. Sometimes helpers (nonbreeding birds) assist in raising the young.
>
> However effective this method of raising young may be, it is not without occasional glitches that point to the species' evolution from a brood parasite. Often the cooperating females attempt to throw each other's eggs out of the nest, just as Old-World cuckoos destroy or eject eggs from the nests they parasitize.

Courtship involves males feeding females as well as occasional reverse mounting. Nests are bulky structures with an inner cup lined with green leaves. The four or five eggs are chalky white. The youngsters remain in the nest for 13 to 14 days and are out and about in another seven days.

These are gregarious birds that rarely are seen alone. On numerous occasions, when finding one crossing a trail or roadway, others will follow. The line of stragglers may stretch out for a minute or more. And when they reach their destination, they greet each other with odd clunking calls. It seems to me that the first in line will stay put until the rest of the flock catches up.

Flocks, sometimes more than two dozen individuals, perch on mid-level branches together overnight. I recall finding a small flock of a dozen or so birds perched in preparation for the night, with their wings spread and tail down. They looked like a bunch of black dishrags sitting in the tree.

When feeding, they often run about on the ground, chasing down insects, such as grasshoppers and crickets, as well as small lizards. And, in season, they will climb into bushes and trees for fruit. Plus, Rylander mentioned that "They have been observed picking external parasites from the backs of cattle."

Timothy Brush, a resident of the Lower Rio Grande Valley, provided the following outlook for groove-billed anis:

> The prospect for Groove-billed Anis in the Valley and Texas as a whole are good. The species seems fairly common in currently protected areas, and anis should be able to use revegetated areas as these mature into thorn forest. Anis seem to be unaffected by the cowbird brood parasitism that has such an impact on many species. Population trends have been generally positive in Texas for the last thirty-five years, as measured by the U.S. Breeding Bird Surveys.

ELEGANT TROGON

This bird is very well-named! It truly is an elegant creature! The male elegant trogon, earlier known as coppery-tailed trogon, has a metallic green head, back, and breast, a rosy red belly and crissum, a white belly band, and a black face and yellow bill. Its long tail is white below and orange-colored above and with a broad black tip. It is spectacular! The female is a brownish version of the male and possesses a small white ear patch behind each eye. Both sit upright in an elegant manner, as if poising for a picture.

In addition, the elegant trogon possesses very distinct vocalizations, a series of loud croaking notes, like rapid "co-ah co-ah co-ah co-ah." Steve Howell and Sophie Webb, in *A Guide to the Birds of Mexico and Northern Central America*, described its voice thusly: "Song (mainly Mar-Aug) a distinctly gruff or hoarse, disyllabic *kwa'h* or *krow'h*, usually repeated 4-6x, also more prolonged series; unlike songs of other trogons. Calls include a rolled chattering *wehrr-rr-rr rr-rr-rr* or *kwerr-rrerrr*, a fairly quiet, steady, gruff *ahrr ahrr…*, and a dry, churring *churrrrrrrr.*" Its calls, resounding in tropical forests, can be ventriloquist.

The elegant trogon is a tropical species that, in the United States, is a breeding bird only in the southern mountains of Arizona. Its range to the south extends to Costa Rica and Guatemala in Central America. My numerous encounters with this trogon have occurred in the Chiricahua and Santa Rita Mountains in southern Arizona, along the Rio Corona in Tamaulipas, in the Sierra Madre Oriental and Sierra Madre Occidental in Mexico, and in the Tikal forest of Guatemala.

My very first encounter with elegant trogons was in 1964 when Bruce Moorhead and I drove from Zion National Park, where we were working at the time, to southern Arizona for the express purpose of seeing a number of birds that were special to that area of the country. During June 8, 9, and 10, we recorded a grand total of 97 species, including elegant trogons in Madera Canyon in the Santa Ritas, a short distance south of Tucson.

I vividly recall my first sighting. While walking along a dry riparian area, with an overstory of cottonwoods, sycamores and other tall trees, I suddenly was looking at a trogon sitting quietly on a branch almost directly overhead. We watched it through binoculars only briefly before it flew up to a round hole in a sycamore. It entered the cavity but almost immediately poked its head back out to see what we were up to. We stared at it for a couple more minutes before it flew out and disappeared up the drainage. Not until then, a couple hundred or more feet away, did it give its hoarse call. It wasn't until then that I realized that I had been hearing that call long before we found it.

My earliest Mexican records of elegant trogons occurred in Tamaulipas. I participated in several Rio Corona Christmas Bird Counts during the late 1970s and early 1980s. I wrote about those counts in *Birder's Mexico*:

> Parrots are everyone's idea of tropical birds. Gehlbach reported four breeding species for the Rio Corona, green and olive-throated parakeets

and red-crowned and yellow-headed parrots. My idea of tropical birds must include the trogon and motmot. Both occur on the Rio Corona. And the name "elegant" trogon is perfect for this gorgeous bird. The male has a brilliant rose-red belly and greenish-gold chest, back, and belly. Its bill is yellow and eye-ring is orange-red. The female is more subtly colored in browns and also has a rosy belly; she has a distinct white ear-patch that is missing on the male.

Until recent years the Rio Corona floodplain was very much intact, but some of the adjacent lands were cleared for agriculture in 1979 and 1980. Since then the floodplain has suffered a fate similar to that of the nearby Rio Purificacion: increased erosion, pollution from chemicals used in agriculture, an increase of exotic nonproductive pants species, and a general loss of native wildlife.

Although elegant trogons nest as far north as Arizona and New Mexico, they cannot survive the colder winters there and must migrate south each year. Fruit is undoubtedly the key to their range; because trogons rely on fruit for their principal food. Mashed insects are fed to their young, but their survival depends upon the availability of fruiting trees, shrubs and vines.

Elegant trogons have also been recorded in the United States at Big Bend National Park in western Texas. During the six years (1966-72) that I worked and lived in the park, I did not see this bird. But I did include the species in *A Field Guide to the Birds of the Big Bend*, thusly:

> Elegant Trogon. *Trogon elegans*. Casual winter and spring visitor. There are only two acceptable reports of this tropical fruit-eater for the park. A female was present in the Chisos Basin from early January to mid-April in 1980. It was first reported along the Window Trail on January 8 by Ron Tiball and party; Norman Scott and Hope Spear also found it that day. The next day, Jerry and Nancy Strickling and Jim Shiflett saw it in the same vicinity. K.H. Husmann next reported it on February 10 near the Chisos Mountains Lodge, and C. L. Sackett, Jr., reported it near the stone cottages on March 9 and 16.

Trogons that nest in the United States and northern Mexico migrate south for the winter months; populations further south are full-time residents. Preferred habitats, in the Arizona mountains as well as in Mexico, include "arid to semiarid woodland, thorn forest, deciduous riparian woods in pine zones," according to Howell and Webb. And Harry Oberholser, writing in *The Bird Life of Texas*, stated:

> It has an extraordinary ability to adapt to a wide variety of vegetation. In Arizona it lives in sycamore and walnut groves beside mountain streams (with or without water); in western Mexico it frequents everything from arid tropical scrub at sea level to pine-oak forests growing between 5,000 and 7,800 feet; in eastern Mexico it inhabits riverside Montezuma baldcypress and strangler figs as well as brush on foothills and lower mountain slopes.

Nesting trogons utilize old woodpecker nests in dead tree trunks and branches from 10 to 20 feet above the ground; some nest sites even occur in rotten and rickety trees. During the early part of the breeding season, they have been observed to occur in single-species flocks or groups of three or four birds; males and females often interact as if paired. Flocks largely consist of males. Both sexes defend their nesting territory against other trogons.

During courtship, male displays include flicking or pumping the tail, inflating his crimson chest while facing his prospective mate, and following the mate from perch to perch while calling constantly. He will lead the female to several possible nest sites, calling from inside each cavity, until she enters an acceptable one.

They enlarge the entrance and cavity with their rather weak bills, she lays three or four eggs in the shallow, unlined cavity; she does the majority of the incubation. The eggs hatch in about two weeks, the nestlings are tended by both parents, and the altricial fledglings are very soon on their own.

In early spring and during the breeding season, trogons are extremely vocal around and about their breeding territory, but usually are less vociferous once eggs are laid. Call notes usually are given leisurely, but at times can be twice the normal speed. And Oberholser mentions that, "when flushed at any time of year, it often utters a low, rapid clucking." He also wrote that

Ordinary flight is slow with deep undulations similar to those of a woodpecker. In feeding, trogons display more dash. They dart out from a limb, hover momentarily before a fruit (often a tropical fig) or an insect on a leaf, quickly snatch the food, then gracefully fly back to the original or to a different perch tree."

While foraging in the lower forest canopy (around 25 feet off the ground), they often sit motionless and scan nearby branches, leaves, and trunk with almost imperceptible movements of the head. When they spot something on a limb or in the air, they burst into flight to catch it by surprise.

The elegant trogon is reasonable common in Mexico, and those in northern Mexico are likely to continue to provide a recruitment base for populations in the U.S. Since most of the trogon habitat in the United States is located in rather isolated mountains, where they are unlikely to be threatened, the species will probably remain safe. However, threats such as those from global warming could affect their essential habitats. Some populations may move to less impacted locations, perhaps into higher locations when possible. Other threats, such as wildfires, related to drying conditions caused by climate change, also are a reality that may significantly impact viable populations.

RINGED KINGFISHER

This is a huge bird, larger than the more common belted kingfisher; it is about the size of a ring-billed gull. It is a colorful bird with a rusty belly and bluish back and crest atop a broad white collar. Its bill is massive, large enough to capture and hold fish the size of small trout; they possess strong black claws. Sexes differ slightly in that the female shows a broad white band between her rusty belly and bluish chest.

Another feature of ringed kingfishers is their very loud vocalizations. Kent Rylander, in *The Behavior of Texas Birds*, wrote that its call is "as single, measured *tzaack*, given loudly in flight; when threatened, this note escalates into a rattle." Steve Howell and Sophie Webb, in *A Guide to the Birds of Mexico and Northern Central America*, described its voice as "A loud, chattering rattle, deeper and often shorter than Belted Kingfisher; also, a gruff, deep *rrruk* in flight, and loud, excited, rough, buzzy, and screechy chatter."

And Harry Oberholser, in *The Bird Life of Texas*, refers to its vocalization as a "rattle-better described as clatters…much lower pitched and heavier than those of the Belted. A loud *kleck kleck kleck kleck* has been described by A. K. Skutch and a rusty *cla-ack*, etc., by F. S. Webster, Jr. The bird vocalizes on the wing and from its perch year-round."

The kingfisher name, according to Paul Ehrlich and colleagues, in *The Birder's Handbook*, "comes from Anglo-Saxon and means "king of the fishes" …The generic name of that kingfisher, *Ceryle*, comes from the Greek for "seabird" or "kingfisher."

World-wide, there are more than 90 species of kingfishers, although there are only five species in North America: belted, ringed, Amazon, green, and American pygmy. Only one – ringed kingfisher – is considered a "borderland" species. Belted kingfishers are widespread, green kingfishers occurs within most of the southern half of Texas, as well as southern Arizona, and Amazon kingfisher is a tropical species that has been found in the U.S. only as an "accidental" vagrant. The American pygmy kingfisher occurs only in southern Mexico and along the coastal plains into Central America.

The range of the ringed kingfisher in the United States is mostly limited to the Rio Grande Valley in south Texas, from about Del Rio to the Gulf of Mexico. It also occurs along a few rivers and streams in the Hill Country in central Texas, and wandering birds have been recorded in West Texas and in Oklahoma, Louisiana, and in western Florida.

Its Hill Country status has been described by Mark Lockwood in *Birds of the Texas Hill Country*, thusly:

> Rare visitor to the southern half of the Edwards Plateau. They are an uncommon permanent resident along the Rio Grande below Lake Amistad in Val Verde County. They may also be rare permanent residents along the Nueces River in Uvalde Cunty and the Guadalupe River in Kerr and Kendall

Counties. Ringed Kingfishers have been found with increasing regularity along the major river systems on the plateau during the past years. The majority of sightings are between mid-September and late April. There are, however, sightings from all months. There has been no evidence of nesting away from the Rio Grande.

Although it is never common, it can be expected along the Rio Grande at such locations as Anzalduas County Park, Bentsen-Rio Grande State Park, Chapéno, Salinéno, and Santa Ana National Wildlife Refuge.

South of the border, ringed kingfishers occur all the way to the tip of South America. In Mexico, they are most common along the Gulf and the Pacific lowlands, as well as the southern half of the Yucatan Peninsula.

All kingfishers are bank-nesters, constructing a tunnel in a river or stream bank where they carve out a nesting chamber at the end. Ringed kingfishers dig a horizontal tunnel up to about eight feet in length. Both parents dig the tunnel and nest chamber. Ehrlich and colleagues stated that they work "alternately, each member of pair emerges from the excavation head-first, removing the detritus piled up by the other."

Harry Oberholser added the following:

Nest in high bank or rivers or canals, but occasionally a long distance from water, usually in brushy or forested regions; sometimes in small colonies; tunnel in the bank, 6 in. in diameter and usually 7-9 ft. long, rising then descending, with an enlarged chamber at end; eggs laid on fish bones and scales.

During courtship, males will circle above their mates and feed them before copulation. She lays four or five eggs and both parents incubate, switching off twice daily. Young are fledged in 34 or 35 days.

Ringed kingfishers are well adapted to life along the riverways, although they also may forage in marine habitats, such as mangroves, and as much as three-quarters of a mile off-shore. They feed on fish and other creatures that are captured underwater or on the shore, such as crabs and crustacea. Their fishing procedure involves spotting prey either by passing over the water or occasionally by hovering, then making quick, headlong dives, sometimes from as much as 40 feet above the surface. Unlike their belted kingfisher cousins, which seldom perch for more than a few seconds while waiting to see prey, ringed kingfishers are far more patient. They may sit still for long periods of time. Once prey is spotted, however, they immediately dive after their prey. They may become completely submerged and stay underwater for several seconds before they literally fly out of the water with a fish held tightly in its bill. They then fly to a perch over the water, where it may beat its prey first before tossing it into the air and swallowing it headfirst. There are times when a fish is so large that it is impossible to swallow and literally sticks out of the bird's throat. To compensate for this situation, these remarkable birds possess very rapid digestion, so that their prey gradually slips into their gut.

Like many other birds that swallow their prey whole, kingfishers regurgitate pellets of undigested materials, bones, and scales

Oberholser (1974) wrote that ringed kingfisher's range is expanding "when practically all other fish-eating birds are declining." He explained:

It is noteworthy that the Texas Ringed Kingfishers reside along the Rio Grande from Falcon Dam (completed in 1953) to mid-Hidalgo County. Apparently, the dam has sufficient held back silt, detergents, and other pollutants from upriver, thereby allowing kingfisher to see their prey in relatively clear, pure water. Also, water going over the spillway picks up oxygen, thus aiding aquatic life downstream. In addition, the river banks in Starr County are high enough for kingfisher nest holes.

ARIZONA WOODPECKER

This woodpecker is another of the Mexican species that barely reaches the United States; it is found only in the southeastern corner of Arizona and the southwestern corner of New Mexico. Its range in Mexico extends along the Sierra Madre Occidental to Jalisco. Habitat preference includes open oak or pine-oak woodlands and open riparian areas dominated with sycamores, all within forests at middle elevations.

Also known as Strickland's woodpecker, this is a medium-sized bird with an all-dark-brown back, white chest and belly with large brown spots, and its head is distinctly marked with white cheeks and a bold, brown patch behind each eye. Males possess a bright red cap that is lacking in females.

Its voice is a "sharp, slightly shrill *chik* or *peek*, a nasal *chriek'a*…usually 2-5 X, and a rapid slightly rough, screeching chatter, gruffer than Ladder-backed Woodpecker," according to Steve Howell and Sophie Webb *in A Guide to the Birds of Mexico and Northern Central America.* Like several other woodpeckers, it is a member of the *Picoides* genus.

The taxonomy of this *Picoides* woodpecker has been rather confusing over the years. At one time both Arizona and Strickland's were lumped *as P. stricklandi*. But the northern birds were split from *stricklandi* and named Arizona woodpecker (*Picoides arizonae*), and Strickland's (also known as brown-backed woodpecker) is *Picoides stricklandi*. So now, *P. stricklandi*, endemic to Mexico, is found only within the volcanic belt from Mexico, D.F. and eastern Michoacán to central Veracruz.

The only place that I have recorded the Arizona woodpecker in the U.S. was in Madera Canyon in the Santa Ritas, just south of Tucson. I remember thinking at first that it was a ladder-backed woodpecker; I had seen that common species earlier. But this bird, about the same size as a ladder-back, had an obviously all-brown back. And I also remember that, unlike ladder-backs, that it usually occurs in open wooded areas; this all-brown-backed Arizona woodpecker seemed almost unwilling to move into more open areas. It apparently preferred the denser oak woodland site along the canyon.

Years later, I found Arizona woodpeckers on several occasions within the Mexican highlands. I wrote about two of those sightings in *Birder's Mexico*; the first was in southern Jalisco:

> Dick Russell and I had driven up the very dusty and winding logging road the day before. We had found the Volcán de Fuego junction on Highway 110, just south of the town of Atenquique, Jalisco, early in the morning of May 4, 1977, and slowly ascended onto the southern flank of this active volcano. We were amazed at the diversity of habitats above the cultivated fields and arid woodlands. The first change was a gradual one of increased tree size and density that produced a good example of tropical deciduous forest habitat. But that zone was little more than a narrow band, because shortly, at about 5,000 feet elevation, we entered a pine forest that looked very similar to the ponderosa pine forests of the southwestern United States. Montezuma and Aztec pines were dominant, but ocote pine (*Pine oocarpa*) was present a well.
>
> I was surprised at the abundance of familiar North American birds that we found during the couple of hours we spent exploring this habitat. I

recorded four woodpeckers (acorn, ladder-backed and Arizona, and northern flicker),…Mexican bird specialties were represented by the russet-crowned motmot, gray-barred and bar-vented wrens, both the rufous-backed and white-throated robins, russet nightingale-thrush, gray silky-flycatcher, rufous-capped warbler, collared towhee, and yellow grosbeak.

In addition to the Jalisco observations, I also wrote about finding an Arizona woodpecker along the forested slopes of Popocatepetl, in central Mexico:

I first birded this habitat just off Highway 190, along the northern edge of the park [Popo-Izta national park] and just east of the Morelos-Mexico state line, on the morning of December 27, 1980. I recorded thirty-one bird species during a two-hour walk through the open forest that reminded me very much of mature ponderosa pine forest in the southwestern part of the United States. The common to fairly common birds recorded included white-eared hummingbird, Strickland's [now Arizona] woodpecker, house (brown-throated) wren, Mexican chickadee, bushtit, white-breasted and pygmy nuthatches, ruby-crowned kinglet; the black-throated green, yellow-rumped, red and olive warblers, and black-headed grosbeak.

The behavior of Arizona woodpeckers is somewhat like that of brown creepers; they actively forage by flying to the base of a tree and then spiral up the trunk feeding conspicuously as they go. And post-nesting birds often join mixed-species flocks that may include chickadees, titmice, nuthatches, and various warblers.

COMMON PAURAQUE

Anyone camping overnight in South Texas will certainly be awakened at dawn by the loud and high-pitched descending "pur-wheeer" or "wheeer" calls of pauraques. All during the years that I camped at Bentsen-Rio Grande Valley State Park in the Lower Rio Grande Valley, or on the Norias portion of the King Ranch, I came to expect and appreciate pauraque's morning chorus. They also possess a call that is a low "chuck chuck" as well as a sustained and eerie toad-like trill. One of the bird's earlier names was "trilling nighthawk." The "wheeer" call sounds somewhat like the Winnie-call of a screech-owl. And when the bird is inactive, it produces a purring sound.

The pauraque is the largest of the goatsuckers of the family Caprimulgidae. It is larger even than the common nighthawk and almost twice the size of the poorwill, the smallest of the goatsuckers. The goatsucker name was derived from the bird's large open mouth that it utilizes to capture large flying insects. It has been reported to even take small bats.

In flight, which seldom occurs above the surrounding brush, its most distinguishing feature is a broad white band across each wing. Its underside is finely banded with brown, its throat is white, and it possesses russet ear patches and large brown eyes. Its beak is extremely short with a sharp, downturned tip

The common pauraque or *curiejo*, is known in Mexico as *tapacaminos picuyo*, and to scientists as *Nyclidromus albicollis*. It is a tropical species that is found in the United States only in Texas. It is most common in the Lower Rio Grande Valley, but its range extends north along the coast and through much of the South Texas brushlands to Choke Canyon and Lake Corpus Christi State Parks and to Aransas National Wildlife Refuge.

South of the border, its range extends along the Gulf Coast, as well as along the Pacific lowlands, south to the Yucatan Peninsula and to northern Argentina. It also is resident on Mexico's Tres Marías, Mujeres, and Cozumel islands.

Preferred habitats were mentioned by Harry C. Oberholser in *The Bird Life of Texas*, thusly:

> The Pauraque inhabits brush country with openings. In far south Texas it is distributed generally over the landscape, but near its northern limit it lives only along tree- and tall-brush-lined rivers. Prime habit is nowadays found in patches of mesquite and Texas ebony woods beside the Rio Grande between Laredo and the delta; likewise, the nearly one-million-acre mesquite-live oak savannah located on the King Ranch between Kingsville and Raymondville is excellent.

Breeding season, at least in the United States, runs from late March to August. Nesting occurs in bushy areas in bottomland woods or on the edges of fields, usually in scattered bushes and cacti. Two eggs are laid on bare ground without any nesting material.

Courtship, according to Paul Ehrlich and colleagues in *The Birder's Handbook*, state that "two birds face each other silently, rock up and down; occ flutter up a few feet flashing white in wings and tail." They also mention that the female will move to another location if disturbed.

The two nestlings are fed by regurgitation by both parents; the adults alternate incubation and brooding every two to three hours; males usually during the morning hours and females at night.

Pauraques fly after dark and spend the daylight hours on the ground in shady brushy areas. It then is so well camouflaged by its brown and black plumage that it is next to impossible to locate. I recall one early morning at Santa Anna National Wildlife Refuge trying to photograph a pauraque that I had seen fly into a brushy area. Although I knew exactly where the bird had entered the site and landed, it took me more than ten minutes to locate the bird it was so well camouflaged. Finally, I found my bird when I detected a blinking eye.

Hunting pauraques hunt either from a low perch or from ground level, flying up to capture low-flying insects. They also are able to run or hop in their efforts to capture prey.

They utilize a wide variety of insects from soft-bodied moths to hard-shelled beetles. However, in order to consume hard-bodied insects they must swallow tiny pebbles that serve a grinding function to ingest insects.

Populations of pauraques are relatively stable throughout their range. The majority of their habitats in the U.S. are seldom disturbed, but that is not always the case south of the border. Perhaps, fire used to clear land for agriculture and grazing is the greatest threat, but the use of pesticides also poses a danger.

BLUE-THROATED AND MAGNIFICENT HUMMINGBIRDS

Blue-throated and magnificent hummingbirds are the two largest hummers in the U.S. Both are about five inches in length, about a third larger than ruby-throats, the most common species in the eastern half of North America. And both are summer residents in the Chisos Mountains of Big Bend National Park, the place where I spent so many marvelous years of my adult life.

The magnificent hummer is the most colorful of the two species. Adult males possess a green back, purple crown, a tiny white spot behind each eye, and a brilliant metallic-green throat. Its breast and upper belly are green, and its tail is dark green and notched. Its voice is a sharp chip and squeaky twitter notes.

The blue-throated hummer is rather dull in comparison with the magnificent, with a mottled green front, a black tail with white corners, and its head is distinctly marked with white eye stripes and a brilliant blue throat. And its voice is loud and distinct. Kent Rylander, in *The Behavior of Texas Birds*, mentioned that it is "The most complex of the hummingbird songs so far studied.

Moreover, the Blue-throated Hummingbird is the hummingbird known in which the female has a complex song."

For me, blue-throated hummingbird calls are representative of the high canyons of the Chisos Mountains. In *A Field Guide to Birds of the Big Bend*, I wrote: "While on its breeding territory, Blue-throats utters loud "seep" notes from a perch and constant "seep, seep, seep" notes in flight; these calls can be heard for a considerable distance. The sharp "chip" of the Magnificent Hummingbird is heard far less often." I also included the following description in my field guide:

> Blue-throated Hummingbird. *Lampornis clemencia.* Fairly common summer resident; casual spring migrant. It can be surprisingly common in Boot Canyon in summer; I counted five pairs along a one-mile stretch on May 9, 1969, and 12 individuals there on August 9, 1969. It is less numerous during dry years. Birds do not arrive on their nesting grounds until early to mid-April, and they usually depart by mid-September; I found only three individuals in Boot Canyon on September 19, 1970...This large hummingbird nests high on Arizona cypress trees along the canyon.

Nests were described by Rylander as "a cup of plain fibers, spiderwebs, and moss placed on sheltered branches or under eaves and bridges. Eggs: incubation by the female, who also cares for the nestlings." He also stated that "this species dominates other hummingbirds and aggressively chases them from favored feeding sites. Their flight is very swift."

I also included the following description of the magnificent hummingbird in my Big Bend field guide:

Magnificent Hummingbird. *Eugenes fulgens*. Uncommon summer resident; casual migrant. It is rarely seen below 6,000 feet...The male Magnificent, unlike the Blue-throat, has no white in the tail. Magnificent Hummers prefer the somewhat higher and drier pinyon-juniper woodlands, whereas Blue-throats are more numerous in the moist canyons. However, Magnificent Hummers often frequent wet areas, especially waterfalls, such as Cattail Falls and the pour-off in Pine Canyon.

Both hummers seem enamored with waterfalls. I included one incident of finding both species, along with a hooded warbler, at the dripping falls in Pine Canyon in *For All Seasons, A Big Bend Journal*, thusly:

April 30 (1969). I found my first hooded warbler in the park this morning in Pine Canyon. It was a gorgeous male with a striking black-and-yellow head pattern. I watched it for several minutes as it walked along the base of the high pour-off that was only dripping water. The bird had found a niche, apparently, with plenty of insects, because it continued feeding all the while I was sitting on a rock about fifty feet away, admiring its colorful plumage and striking behavior.

Also, at the dripping water that morning was a pair of blue-throated hummingbirds and a single male magnificent hummingbird. All three of these large hummers were fly-catching along the high rock pour-off. They spend considerable time flying up and down the cliff face in search of insects that apparently were attracted to the available water.

One of the northernmost locations for these two hummers is the Guadalupe Mountains of southern New Mexico and Texas. I wrote about my observations of these two birds in Guadalupe Mountains National Park in *Birding the Southwestern National Parks*, thusly:

> Hummingbirds can be common along the canyon, and once century plants begin to flower, they provide a showplace for these brightly colored Lilliputians. One June morning I sat in the shade of a Gambel's oak and, through my binoculars, watched hummingbirds feeding on the flowers of a nearby New Mexico agave. Black-chinned Hummingbirds were most numerous, distinguished by a purple-black chin contrasting with a white chest. Broad-tailed Hummingbirds were common as well and easy to identify by the males' trilling wing beats and rosy-red throats. Two larger hummers also put in their appearance during my hour-long vigil: Blue-throated and Magnificent.

> I detected the presence of the Blue-throated Hummingbird before I actually observed it because of its loud "seep" calls made in flight. When it finally approached the yellow flowers, its size was striking in comparison with the smaller Black-chins hovering nearby. The male's bright blue throat and the white corners of its tail were also evident. But the hummingbird of the day was the equally large Magnificent Hummingbird, which suddenly appeared as if by magic. Its deep green back and throat patch, shiny black belly, and purple crown gleamed in the morning sunlight like a bright jewel. It stayed only a few seconds before flying off with rather heavy wing beats, almost directly over where I stood in admiration.

Although I had seen this bird several times before in the Chisos Mountains of Big Bend National Park, the McKittrick Canyon sighting was one of the most memorable. I have seen it in McKittrick Canyon several times since then; despite being at the northern edge of its breeding range, this is the best place in Texas to find this tropical species

These two large hummers barely reach the United States where Mexico's Sierra Madre Occidental enters into Arizona and where Mexico's Sierra Madre Oriental enters into Texas. The Mexican range of the blue-throated hummer follows the mountains almost to the Isthmus of Techantepec, while the range of the magnificent hummer extends southward to northern South America.

I have recorded both of these hummers at numerous locations in Mexico. Three encounters stand out: The Sierra de Autlán in Jalisco, the El Triunfo area in Chiapas, and near treeline on Pico de Orizaba. I wrote about these occurrences in *Birder's Mexico*.

Above La Cumbre in the Sierra de Autlán, I followed a trail that skirted a large canyon to a rather impressive oak woodland. It was there that "I recorded a total of seventy-four birds from along the trail; several of these were Mexican species of special interest. Four were hummers: the long-tailed hermit, berylline, violet-crowned and magnificent hummingbirds."

At El Triunfo, some of the birds about our camp included "band-tailed pigeon, white-tipped dove, singing quail, mottled and fulvous owls, violet sabrewing, green-throated mountain-gem, magnificent hummingbird, mountain trogon, emerald toucanet, hairy and golden-olive woodpeckers, both the spotted and spot-crowned woodcreepers, scaly-throated and ruddy foliage-gleeners," etc.

My third encounter occurred during a day-long hike on Pico de Orizaba:

I climbed to the summit of an isolated hill, situated just below the forest that formed a line of vegetation below timberline, to get to a good view of the surrounding landscape. It was well worth the time and energy. The view alone, toward the snow-covered peak that formed a magnificent backdrop to the forests and fields, made the entire day worthwhile.

We found forty-two bird species that day. Although many of those were the same as are mentioned above for Popo, we found a few others too. The most interesting of these were blue-throated hummingbird, a lone violet-green swallow, both Steller's and gray-breasted jays, bridled titmouse, hermit and Townsend's warblers, collared towhee, rufous-capped brush-finch, and black-headed siskin.

Ever since my Big Bend years, the blue-throated hummingbird has been extra special to me. So, when the University of Texas Press decided to publish a series of paintings by John P. O'Neill, editor Suzanne Winkler asked me to write a sidebar for John's painting of "Blue-throated Hummingbird and Claret Cup Cactus." A portion of that offering follows:

The loud, continuous *seep seep seep* of a male Blue-throated Hummingbird dominated the canyon. I searched the high foliage of an Arizona cypress, trying to find the perpetrator, without success. Its loud song continued. Finally, I moved a short distance up the slope behind me, above the wooded canyon to where I could see the top of the high cypress. There it was, sitting in the open at the very top, proclaiming to all the world, especially to any other blue-throated males that might be in the area, that it was "king of the hill."

The male Blue-throated Hummingbird suddenly took wing, diving down in hot pursuit of a passing Broad-tailed Hummingbird that, apparently, had unknowingly invaded its territory. I could hear the blue-throat's constant seep notes for a surprising distance as it pursued the smaller hummingbird down Boot Canyon.

LUCIFER HUMMINGBIRD

During the six years (1966-72) that I worked at Big Bend National Park, I lived in national park housing at Panther Junction, behind and uphill from the visitor center. I established a banding station behind my house, and I hung two hummingbird feeders just outside my back windows. Those two feeders became the most reliable place in the park to see lucifer hummingbirds. Dozens of birders were able to see lucifers there; they were lifers for many.

A few years later, after experiencing the park and its birdlife, I wrote *A Field Guide to Birds of The Big Bend*, in which I included the following discussion about lucifer hummingbirds:

> Lucifer Hummingbird. *Calothorax lucifer*. Fairly common spring, summer, and fall resident. This little hummingbird with a decurved bill arrives in the park as early as March 8 and has been recorded as late as November 10; a May 7, 1901 report for the Chisos Basin by the U.S. Biological Survey was the first ever in the United States (Bailey 1905). During May, except on the Rio Grande floodplain, where Black-chins are more plentiful, it may be the hummer most commonly seen from the desert lowlands to the highest slopes of the Chisos Mountains. And when century plants are in bloom, usually from May through September, lucifers can be found with patience, at just about any plant. Joe Kuban's study of hummingbirds in the Chisos Mountains (1977) suggested that lucifers do better during dry years when Black-chin numbers are reduced.

The word lucifer is Latin and can be translated as "beautiful-breasted light-bearer," referring to the male's beautiful, shiny gorget. The lucifer hummingbird is best identified by its decurved bill, the male's plumage is unique due to its exquisite, broad and elongated purple gorget, green crown, buff flanks, and long, forked, purplish tail. In sunlight, its gorget can shine like a bright jewel. Females are similar but lack the purple gorget. In flight, it produces a steady humming sound. And its voice often is a loud, shrill squeak. Gary Clark, in *Book of Texas Birds*, described its voice as "Chip sounds by males, females, and immatures. Chip-trill sounds at nest or near feeding territory. Males often a *brrzhee! brrzhee!* sound when on territory or if another male is around."

Blooming century plants attract a wide variety of wildlife each June and July. I recall sitting along Oak Creek one morning for about two hours watching the activity at a huge, blooming century plant. I recorded a grand total of fourteen birds and two mammals – rock and antelope squirrels - that were utilizing the plant and/or its platter-size yellow flowers in one way or another. Birds included nectar-feeders, insect-feeders, and a few that were simply using the tall plant as a resting or singing post.

Three species of hummingbirds – lucifer, blue-throated, and broad-tailed – came to sip the sweet nectar from the bright yellow flowers. Each remained for only a few seconds before flying off on other pursuits. A pair of Scott's orioles visited the flowers on two occasions, and an immature male also came by for a quick visit. White-winged doves were present most of the time, but I never was sure whether I was watching two or three individuals that returned after brief absences or if each visit represented a different bird.

Lucifers are Mexican species that barely enter the United States at two locations: the Texas Big Bend area and southwestern New Mexico/southeastern Arizona where they are a rare summer visitor. However, they can be expected with regularity only in Texas.

This species previously was considered to be quite rare within the Big Bend, the only place in the United States where it had been recorded regularly. However, it can be reasonably common. In May, except for black-chinned hummingbirds on the Rio Grande floodplain and broad-tails in the mountain woodlands, it may be the most commonly seen hummingbird from the Rio Grande to the highest slopes of the Chisos Mountains.

In Mexico, the range of the lucifer hummingbird extends south almost to Mexico City, the same general range as the Chihuahuan Desert; lechuguilla is the indicator plant. Lucifers are a fairly common to common breeder throughout, and U.S. breeders join the Mexican resident birds during the winter months.

The first U.S. lucifer hummingbird nest was discovered on a lechuguilla stalk by Warren Pulich and son near Terlingua on July 13, 1982, and Peter Scott later located 24 nests between Panther Junction and the Chisos Basin. Along with ocotillo and cholla, a few of the 24 nests were situated on lechuguilla stalks. The tiny lucifer nests are constructed of soft natural plant materials and bound together with spider silk and camouflaged with lichens.

Lucifer courtship and nesting were described by Kent Rylander in *The Behavior of Texas Birds:*

The male displays while the female builds the nest and incubates the eggs. He makes short flights back and forth between two perches, with much rustling of the wings. He concludes his display by spiraling high into the air, diving steeply past the nest, then performing a series of pendulum swings in front of his mate.

Nests: often in a cholla, agave, or ocotillo, up to 5,000 feet in elevation; it is a cup that the female constructs from plant fibers and decorates with leaves. Eggs: incubation by the female, who also feeds the nestlings. In spite of the demands of feeding the first brood, she sometimes lays a second clutch before the first fledglings have left the nest. Both parents aggressively defend their nestlings and feeding territories.

Post-nesting lucifers frequent the mountain canyons where they feed on the bright red flowers of mountain sage; I counted eight males and seven females in Boot Canyon on August 9, 1969. By late August, however, highland birds begin to move to lower elevations. They usually can then be found in the lower mountain canyons until the second week of September, when there is a noticeable decline. From early October to November, remaining birds frequent the lower parts of the desert and along the Rio Grande, where they feed on flowering tree tobacco plants.

Harry Oberholser, in the *Bird Life of Texas*, provides us with a general statement about lucifer's daily activities:

During the course of the hummer's day it sips much nectar from flowers and catches tiny insects (frequently gnats and small flies) in the air; beelike, the bird also fertilizes plants by transporting pollen on its bill and forehead to the flowers it visits…Migration flight speed is usually near 20 m.p.h. On gauzelike wings the birds buzz to, hover before, probe with their bills, and then backs away from spring flowers.

In May 1967, I established a banding station at the cabin at Boot Spring. I wrote about banding hummers at the cabin in *For All Seasons, A Big Bend Journal*:

May 25 (1967). I spent the night in the cabin at Boot Spring and after supper walked to the South Rim to watch the sunset. Storm clouds to the west obliterated the normally outstanding sunset, but the early darkness apparently triggered night-bird activity. Walking the 1.8-mile trail back to the cabin after dark, I recorded four whip-poor-wills, two common poorwills, two flammulated owls, and one eastern screech-owl.

I set up three mist nets near the cabin at 10:00 p.m. and on checking them at midnight found that I had captured a pair of flammulated owls (undoubtedly two additional birds from those I had heard earlier). I measured and banded both individuals, released them, folded up the nets and went back to bed.

I got up before dawn, unfolded the nets, and fixed breakfast. An hour later, on checking the nets, I found that I had caught eight hummingbirds: two male and five female broad-tails and one male magnificent. I slowly untangled the hummingbirds and released them, one at a time. But as soon as I released the first one, rather than flying out of harm's way as expected, it remained near the net, buzzing me and seemingly trying to help its companions. Each of the released hummers joined the first one in an apparent state of agitation, diving at me and hovering nearby until all the birds were released. At least four additional hummers, including a pair of blue-throats and a female lucifer, joined the agitated throng. I can't imagine what else these birds were up to if not defending their fellow hummingbirds.

I recall another spring day in Coahuila, Mexico where I spend time birding along a dry wash, identifying the various trees and shrubs. Two desert plants in particular that day included the yellow trumpet and desert willow. Sometimes they are confused with legumes, because of their pod-like beans, but instead are members of the catalpa family. Yellow trumpet, called *esperanza* or *tronadiro* in Spanish, is common in desert washes.

Sitting in the shade of an adjacent honey mesquite eating lunch, I watched four species of hummers – broad-billed, lucifer, black-chinned and broad-tailed – feeding at the large purplish-red blossoms of a desert willow. It seemed to me that the lucifer hummer had an advantage in obtaining nectar from the large blossoms due to its decurved bill; it seemed able to probe deeper than the straight-billed birds.

Essential habitats for lucifer hummingbirds are reasonably secure. Their arid and usually isolated locations are rarely subject to pressures from agriculture and/or grazing.

I cannot help but wonder, however, what effects global warming will have on this little desert hummer. Will the range of ocotillo and lechuguilla eventually creep northward to allow lucifers that depend upon those plants for nesting to move northward, or will increasing droughts have a negative influence on their well-being?

BUFF-BELLIED HUMMINGBIRD

This large hummingbird may be one of the numerous birds that has moved north in recent years due to climate change. Several years ago, while working at Big Bend National Park, I drove down to the Lower Rio Grande Valley to see some of that area's specialty birds, those not found anywhere else in the United States. One of my target birds was the buff-bellied hummingbird. Even there, however, I had to go to one special location, a private backyard in McAllen, to see this bird. I did see it there, but I did not see it again all during the week I was birding in the Valley; at that time, it was considered a Mexican species that only occasional was found north of the border.

After retiring from the National Park Service in 1989 and moving to Victoria, Texas, I learned that there was a single location just outside of Victoria where buff-bellies could be seen. I visited that site and did see that bird. I was told by the lady that owned the property that buff-bellies had appeared only a few years earlier. And, within four or five years I discovered this hummer in my own yard in the fall; it remained there for a few months and then disappeared. I assumed that it had come north, like so many other birds as a post-nesting vagrant, and then returned to its breeding grounds south of the border or in the Lower Rio Grande Valley. But it was only a few years later that buff-bellies became a full-time resident in my Victoria yard, and then there was never a time that I could not find one or several of these hummers among the oaks in my backyard.

Buff-bellied hummers are one of our largest hummingbirds at about four and a half inches in length and weighing four to five grams. In North America, only the blue-throated and magnificent hummingbirds are larger. But both of those hummers, primarily Mexican species, occur only in the mountains of western Texas and southern Arizona. Buff-bellies are generally thought of as a tropical species, reaching the United States only in the South Texas area.

The buff-bellied hummingbird is our only resident hummingbird with a red bill; it also is distinguished be an emerald green throat, buff underparts, and a rufous tail. Timothy Brush, in *Nesting Birds of a Tropical Frontier*, described it further:

> As with most hummingbirds, seeing the iridescent bright colors depends on the light and the angle at which one sees the bird. In shade, the Buff-bellied appears dark and seems to disappear into the thickets it inhabits, while in a straight-up sunlit view the greenish head, back, and throat glisten. The throat of adult males shows a bluish tinge overlaying the green. The somewhat forked, rust-colored tail is also striking, although not iridescent. Perhaps the bird should have been named Rufous-tailed Hummingbird, but that

name was already in use for *A. tzacatl*. The buffy-colored belly is not very noteworthy, but it does help distinguish this species from similar species.

Buff-bellies possess a unique voice, a high-pitched metallic or shrill squeaky note. Some of these can be loud and piercing, especially during courtship or when a bird is defending its territory. Brush interprets this call as "*Tikk. Tikk. Tikk.*" Although the sexes are marked alike, adult males are somewhat brighter with a redder bill.

Buff-bellies were earlier known as fawn-breasted or Yucatan hummingbirds, the latter name in recognition of their type locality. Its scientific name is *Amazilia yucatanensis*. But none of these names does justice to these birds, which are among our most colorful and personable hummers. And it may seem odd, but hummingbirds, members of the Family Trochilidae, are very closely related to swifts, according to ornithologists.

Buff-bellied hummingbirds are tropical hummers that range as far south as Guatemala but only north to South Texas and along the edge of the Central Texas plains during their breeding season. But this has not always been the case. Only since the 1970s have they been recorded regularly north of the Lower Rio Grande Valley. By the early 1900s they had moved northward in the Upper Texas Coast, and since the late 1990s have become a fulltime resident.

Preferred habitats include oak mottes, thickets, and citrus groves, although nesting can occur on a variety of trees and shrubs. In the fall of 1995, I discovered a deserted buff-belly nest hanging on a yaupon branch in my yard. Like all hummingbird nests, this one was constructed of plant fibers and decorated with lichens and bound with spider webbing. Fresh hummingbird nests are little more than thimble-size, but by the time the young are fledged the nests usually have been stretched to twice the original size. Female buff-bellies build the nests and incubates the two all-white eggs, but both parents feed the nestlings.

Buff-bellies have a bold and assertive personality. Males often perch in open trees within easy viewing of a feeder or patch of flowering plants. On numerous occasions I have found buff-bellies sitting in trees in my yard or directly over a patch of flowering Turk's-caps in Santa Ana National Wildlife Refuge in the Valley; they seem to have an affinity for large tubular flowers. They may sit for long periods, watching whatever is moving in their surroundings, and then suddenly, without warning, they will streak off to another perch or after another hummingbird, a territorial invader. Or they may dive down to sip liquid from a feeder or flower, and then, after feeding a short time, will return to a favorite perch.

Naturalist Louis J. Halle had a deep appreciation of hummingbirds. He wrote:

> I have always felt that the hummingbird was a special gift to the New World… The human imagination, which created unicorn, dragon, and phoenix, has created nothing more wondrous. It is like a precious gem, emerald or ruby, that has life and movement, that hovers, dips, and darts in the air. Looking only at its form and color, its jeweled surface, one would say it belongs in a prince's turban. Its wings have more delicacy than the finest watchwork,

humming when they set off, whirring so fast they are blurred to sight, shooting it here and there, back and forth, or holding stationary in the air.

Buff-bellied hummingbirds are a true wonder, and one of the many birds found in South Texas that attracts birders and other nature lovers to the Valley for the joy of watching this brightly colored and active hummingbird.

WHITE-EARED HUMMINGBIRD

I included my very first-ever white-eared hummingbird sighting in *For All Seasons A Big Bend Journal*:

August 13 (1966). Today, I found my very first white-eared hummingbird. A lifer! Boot Canyon was full of bird song when I arrived at about 10 a.m. I walked up canyon toward the South Rim, watching for any birds and other wildlife that might appear. Several northbound migrants, including rufous hummingbirds and Townsend's, black-throated gray, and Wilson's warblers, were present, feeding in the oks and maples along the canyon bottom. Hummingbirds were also taking advantage of the red-flowering mountain sage that dotted the adjacent slopes.

I found the white-eared hummingbird, a brightly marked male, along the east-facing slope above the check-dam. It, too, was sampling the mountain sage nectar. Its bold white eyeline, short red bill with a black tip, and deep purple-black chin and crown were obvious in the late morning light. It continued to feed at one of several mountain sages, allowing me a wonderful view for several minutes. This is a relatively small hummer, compared with the more common broad-tailed and even larger blue-throated hummingbirds that also were present along the canyon. Through binoculars, its square, rather stubby, two-tone (black and green) tail was obvious. At one time during my observations it uttered a metallic chattering call, as if it had found an especially sweet flower. I later learned that my white-eared hummingbird, normally found only in the Mexican highlands, was one of the first ever recorded in Texas; I found the species only twice in six years.

The voice of the white-eared hummer was more fully described by Steve Howell and Sophie Webb in *A Guide to The Birds of Mexico and Northern Central America*, thusly: "Song, a tedious, metallic chipping, *chi'tink chi'tink ch'tink* …or *chi'fit chi'dit chi'dit* … or simply *tink tink*…etc.; lacks hesitant, jerky rhythm typical of Green Violet-ear. Fairly hard, dry chips, at times repeated steadily, may break into short, quiet gurgles."

Howell and Webb also provided a description of the white-ears' preferred Mexican habitat: "Pine-oak, oak, and pine-evergreen forest, clearings with flowers. Feeds and perches at low to mid-levels, often abundant along low banks of flowers."

Their diet also includes small insects, either captured in flight or gleaned off bark, leaves and other surfaces.

Several years after my first white-eared sighting at Big Bend, I wrote a bird field guide for Big Bend National Park. I included the white-eared hummingbird in my "Annotated List of Species," thusly:

White-eared Hummingbird *Hylocharis leucotis*. Rare summer visitor. A female, collected by Tarleton Smith in the Chisos Mountains on July 7, 1937, represented the first Texas record of this species. It has since been reported in the mountains on numerous occasions between April 27 and September 1; there are no indications of nesting. Records more than likely are spring wanderers and post-nesting vagrants. Most sightings are in July and early August at mountain sage, blooming on the high slopes; there also are a few reports in and about the Chisos Basin.

Big Bend National Park holds the record for the greatest number of hummingbird species recorded in any of America's national parks, fifteen. White-eared and broad-billed hummers visit the park only in the fall, but known nesters include broad-tailed, blue-throated, magnificent, lucifer, and black-chinned. Ruby-throated, Anna's, Costa's, calliope, and rufous hummers are only migrants or occasional fall visitors. And there are single records of berylline and violet-crowned hummingbirds.

White-eared hummingbirds are tropical species that reach the United States only at the extreme northern edge of their range at Big Bend, but as casual visitors only. Their range south of the border follows the Sierra Madre Occidental and Sierra Madre Oriental to the Isthmus, and it also occurs in northern Central America.

I have recorded white-ears several times in Mexico, and mentioned some of those sightings in *Birder's Mexico*. One of those sighting was at La Cubre in the Sierra de Autlan:

> We found five hummingbirds along the upper trail, two of which were priority birds in our search. We discovered that the one lifer, the amethyst-throated hummingbird was fairly common, but we found only one crowned woodnymph. The other three hummers seen were the white-eared, blue-throated, and magnificent. All mountain species we found fairly common at all of the highland localities we birded.

The behavior of white-eared hummers was described by Harry Oberholser in *The Bird Life of Texas*:

> The precision flight and pugnacious behavior of this bird are typical of the family. Often joining other hummers, White-ears cluster around an agave, scarlet bouvardia, or other flowering plant where, in between bickering and sparring, they sip nectar and eat insects. Unlike hummingbirds in general, which are reputed to prefer red, the White-ear is strongly attracted to blue flowers, especially those of *Salvia mexicana*.

BROAD-BILLED HUMMINGBIRD

One warm May day in Coahuila, while eating lunch in the shade of an adjacent honey mesquite, I watched four species of hummingbirds – broad-billed, lucifer, black-chinned, and broad-tail – feeding at the large purplish-red blossoms of a desert willow. I later wrote about that day and the flowering shrubs that were being utilized by the hummers in *Birder's Mexico*:

> Two desert plants that are sometime confused with legumes, because of their pod-like beans, but instead are members of the catalpa family, are yellow trumpet and desert willow. These are two of my personal favorites… Desert willow is restricted to desert washes, and I have discovered that it is a real favorite of hummingbirds.

The broad-billed hummingbird is another of the Mexican specialties that barely reach the United States in southeastern Arizona, where it nests, and in Big Bend National Park, where it is a casual visitor only. However, there is one record of nesting: Roy Quillen discovered a nest containing eggs at the Johnson Ranch on May 17, 1934.

My only sighting of this hummer in the United States was at Big Bend National Park, a lone male in Boot Canyon on August 7, 1969. I included it in *A Field Guide to Birds of the Big Bend,* and wrote that it is a "casual summer resident, and spring and fall visitor."

South of the border, its range extends along the western slope of the country almost to the Isthmus; it does not occur within the northeastern portion of Mexico.

This is a gorgeous little hummer with white obvious undertail coverts and a red bill. Steve Howell and Sophie Webb provided a further description in *A Guide to the Birds of Mexico and Northern Central America*:

> Bill bright red with black tip. Throat glittering blue to violet-blue, underparts glittering blue-green, undertail coverts white, often with dusky centers, to dusky with whitish edgings. Crown, nape, and upperparts emerald green. Tail blue-black, inner rectrices tipped greyish. Female bill blackish above, red below with dark tip. White postocular stripe contrasts with dull green crown and blackish auriculares. Nape and upperparts emerald green to golden green. Throat and upperparts pale grey to dusky grey. Tail variable, typically emerald green to blue-green (rarely blue-black), outer rectrices with fairly broad blue-black terminal band, tipped white.

The voice a broad-billed hummer was described by Harry Oberholser in *The Bird Life of Texas*, as "The chattering notes suggest those of a Ruby-crowned Kinglet. As with most hummers, calls are frequent when individuals are feeding and sparring on the wing; these activities continue all year." Oberholser also mentions that the

Flight of the Broadbill, especially as it flashes from flower to flower, appears somewhat jerkier and more irregular than that of other hummers. Also, the species at times seems to be quieter and less active; individuals often perch on a dead twig in more open places, even on top of a tree, where they can survey their surroundings."

Jim Peterson and Barry Zimmer later (1998), in *Birds of the Trans Pecos*, summarized its status in Texas, as "Casual at all seasons, with scattered records throughout. There are some historical records from the 1930s and 1940s in Big Bend country, but no nesting has occurred recently."

ROSE-THROATED BECARD

An adult male rose-throated becard is a big-headed bird with a brushy crest. About the size of a large sparrow, it is distinctly marked with its bright rose-colored throat, against a whitish chin and belly, and grayish-black head, back and tail. Females are overall brown, except for a black cap. In good sunlight their back can be a pale orange color.

Rose-throat vocalizations, although seldom heard, were described by Steve Howell and Sophie Webb in *A Guide to the Birds of Mexico and Northern Central America*:

> A plaintive, down-slurred *t-sseu* or *tzeeu*, and a shorter *sseeu* or *teew*, often run into a reedy, rolled, sputtering chatter or trill, or a chatter may slur into a plaintive *tcheu* or *tew*. In alarm near nest, a quiet *pik* and *pii-dik*. Rarely heard dawn song a slightly reedy, plaintive *si-tchew wii-chew*, or si-tseeu *wii-tzeeu*, repeated, at times *si-seeu wii-tzee, si tseeu*, etc.

The rose-throated becard (*Pachyramphus aglaiae*) is a member of the Cotingidae Family which includes twelve species, although the rose-throat is the only one that has been recorded in the United States. The eleven other family members include the cinnamon, white-winged, and grey-collared becards; thrushlike and speckled mourners; masked and black-crowned tityras; grey-headed piprites (manakin); rufous piha; lovely cotinga; and three-wattled bellbird. Most of these are rather drab birds with little color, but exceptions, besides the rose-throated becard, include the black-and-white masked tityra, with its red bill and eye ring, and the brightly-colored lovely cotinga. A male lovely cotinga, with its turquoise-blue and black plumage, is one of the most striking birds in all of Mexico.

Rose-throated becards are tropical birds found principally in the arid riparian forests, open woodlands, and mangroves of Mexico and adjacent Costa Rica. Their rare occurrence in the United States usually is as a post-nesting visitor. But there are a few documented nesting records from the 1940s through the 1970s. Their status in the U.S. was described by Mark Lockwood and Brush Freeman in their 2004 *Handbook of Texas Birds*, thusly:

> Very rare and irregular visitor to the Lower Rio Grande Valley, primarily Hidalgo County. Rose-throated Becards were formerly a rare and local resident in the Lower Rio Grande Valley, limited to Cameron and Hidalgo Counties. Since the mid-1970s, there have been 20 documented records for the state, the majority between early December and mid-March. Since 1980s, very few summer records exist, and the only nesting attempts (all unsuccessful) occurred at Anzalduas County Park and Santa Ana National Wildlife Refuge, Hidalgo County.

The rose-throated becard also occurs in southern Arizona where it was earlier known as Xantus' becard. Habitats in both areas are similar. They include riparian zones with tall trees often with overlapping canopies. South of the border, however, they also utilize "forest edge, including pine-oak clearings, open areas with scattered trees and hedges, riparian groves," according to Howell and Webb.

Their presence in southern Arizona and southeastern Texas undoubtedly is due to populations in nearby Mexico. River corridors from the south, such as Sonoita Creek near Patagonia, Arizona, and Rio Corona below the Lower Rio Grande Valley in Texas, provide routes for recruitment. Post-nesting movement, especially for immature birds, is most likely the reason for their presence north of the border.

Santa Ana National Wildlife Refuge, in the Lower Rio Grande Valley, has long been one of my favorite birding sites. As early as the mid-1960s, while working at Big Bend National Park, I would drive to the Valley, camp at Bentsen-Rio Grande Valley State Park, and bird the Valley. It was during those visits when I found many birds that were lifers at the time.

My first and only sighting of a rose-throated becard in the United States was not at Santa Ana or Bentsen, but at nearby Anzalduas County Park. Another birder at Bentsen told me about a rumor of a becard at Anzalduas, so I spend the next morning there searching for the bird. I eventually found a pair of birds and a partially-constructed nest.

The female becard was the only bird that appeared to be building the nest; the male becard seemed to be more of a watcher than an active participant. I spent more than an hour watching the nest-building activities and not once did I see the male being more than a casual observer.

Timothy Brush, in *Nesting Birds of a tropical Frontier*, reported on becards at Anzalduas as follows:

> In 1999, a female becard built at least one nest at Anzalduas in the absence of a male, between May 8 and June 3. A subadult male was first seen at Anzalduas on June 3, and he immediately paired with the female. I suspected that incubation was under way during June, but the nest was abandoned by June 24. The becards built a second nest between June 24 and July 2, with the female doing most of the work, but it also was abandoned, July 15. Female Bronzed Cowbirds were observed approaching each nest on one occasion, but it is not known if nests were parasitized.

Brush's examples of unsuccessful nesting probably are typical of rose-throated becards north of the border. Although the habitat in the Lower Rio Grande Valley may be adequate, at least in comparison with nearby habitats in Mexico, such as the riparian corridor along the Rio Corona, northern nesting success is few and far between. And with climate change and increasing droughts, further nesting success in the U.S. is doubtful.

Rose-throated becard nests seem much larger than one would expect for such a small bird. They are a large cylindrical heap of vegetable matter woven about a group of terminal twigs on a high, outreaching limb of a tall cottonwood or sycamore where it can sway freely in the breeze. Harry Oberholser, in *Bird Life of Texas*, wrote that they belonged in the "splendid weaving category." And according to Allan Phillips, in describing an Arizona nest in a 1949 article in the journal *The Condor*, he wrote:

> The binding material is composed mainly of long strips of inner bark taken from dead cottonwood limbs, interwoven with quantities of grass, leaves, patches of insect webs, rootlets, and other miscellaneous materials. The lining of a fallen nest contained some contour feathers, while in the outer parts may be found occasional quills, mostly of Band-tailed Pigeon. The nesting cup is well inside the structure.
>
> Nests vary considerably in outside dimensions, ranging from 12 to 25 or 30 inches high (long) and from 10 to 12 in general diameter. They may be anything from spherical to rather pear-shaped in outline, and are placed from 30 to 60 feet above the ground.

The typical feeding behavior of becards is a sit-and-wait method, watching for insects and other arthropods that might pass by or can be gleaned from the adjacent vegetation. They also feed on various fruits, seeds, and berries, such as figs. Becards also hawk insects like flycatchers.

For the most part, becards are quiet mannered birds that spend much of their time in the upper foliage of trees. That behavior usually makes them difficult to find. However, in quiet areas, not subject to rushing waters, I have found the species by its sharp "tsee" or its very high-pitched "tee-tee-tee" calls. And after locating one, they often seem to ignore the observer. Phillips described its "rather long drawn out and descending whistle closely resembles that of a Gray Hawk." And Howell and Webb claim that it also has a "rarely heard dawn" call that is slightly reedy, plaintive "si-chew wii-chew" or "si-tseeu wiltzee."

Although the rose-breasted becard is considered a full-time resident wherever it occurs, some ornithologists believe it to be a migrant. Some populations, including those in the Chiriquí highlands of Panama, do experience a post-nesting movement, that is particularly true for immature males.

I have encountered rose-throated becards within a variety of areas in Mexico. These range from the lowlands along the Rio Corona in Tamaulipas to the highlands of the Sierra Madre Occidental. For example, while searching for tufted jays in Durango, I discovered a nesting pair of rose-throated becards on a forested slope just above a canyon bottom. I wrote about that encounter in *Birding Mexico*:

> We walked further up the canyon to where it became more of an upland slope than a canyon bottom. At the far end we found a pair of rose-throated becards attending a nest hanging from the bare limb of what I believe was a hackberry tree. The rose-pink throat patch of the male was truly iridescent that day. And although I had seen this species many times before, both in the United States and Mexico, I had never seen the brilliance of the throat color as it was that day.

Other Mexican species recorded that day in the immediate vicinity included white-throated robins, happy wren, three hummingbirds – white-eared, berylline and cinnamon – and an ivory-billed woodcreeper.

There is an additional becard in Jamaica, the Jamaican becard. It is similar to the rose-breasted becard, but the male Jamaican becard is entirely black and is "sleeker, with a longer, thinner and more pointed bill and a smaller head," according to Herbert Raffaele and colleagues, in *A Guide to the Birds of the West Indies*. I recorded this Jamaican endemic in the Blue Mountain highlands, as mentioned in my *A Birder's West Indies, An Island by Island Tour*. It was associated with "several Ring-tailed Pigeons, a Jamaican Woodpecker and the little Jamaican Euphonia."

Observing a rose-throated becard in the United States usually depends upon the unlikely possibility of a stray bird in south Texas or in southern Arizona. True serendipity!

THICK-BILLED KINGBIRD

The thick-billed kingbird is a Mexican bird whose breeding grounds barely reaches the United States in southern Arizona, extreme southwestern New Mexico, and the Texas Big Bend country. I wrote about my initial sightings of a thick-billed kingbird at Big Bend National Park in *For All Seasons, A Big Bend Journal*:

> June 21 (1967). "Ro, some folks at the information desk are reporting a thick-billed kingbird in the Basin. Do you want to talk with them?" Seasonal naturalist Dick Nelson, who had been working at the Panther Junction Visitor Center desk, had talked with the Hendersons who were reporting their find. He had decided that the report was probably valid and that I would be interested. I immediately left my stack of paperwork and went to the front desk to talk with the Hendersons. Since there were no previously confirmed records of this flycatcher in Texas, it was of considerable interest.
>
> It was soon obvious that Mr. and Mrs. O. R. Henderson, of Clearwater, Florida, were experienced birders and that they were aware of the significance of their find. They had, in fact, already photographed the bird and agreed to send me a copy for documentation. Although the Hendersons were leaving the park, they gave me good directions on where to find this bird in the Chisos Basin.
>
> Within about two hours, Dick Nelson and I had driven to the Basin, walked about one mile down the Window Trail to the approximate location, and were watching a real live thick-billed kingbird. For the next three hours we observed this bird, which remained within an area of about twenty-five

acres. On numerous occasions it would dash out after a passing insect, which it usually caught with a loud snap of its huge, all black bill. It called loud "kiterrer" and "cut-a-reep" notes on several occasions. Once it chased a passing violet-green swallow for several hundred feet before returning to its perch.

We left our post at 2:00 p.m., but when I returned during the early evening hours, I was unable to locate the bird again. Several weeks later, I received a slide from the Hendersons of a thick-billed kingbird, sitting on the open branches of its Chisos Mountains perch. I included the photograph with a short article that appeared in the *Southwestern Naturalist* [scientific journal] in December 1967.

I next recorded a thick-billed kingbird in the park near San Vicente along the River Road on May 25, 1971. And one also spent the winter near Boquillas Canyon where it was seen numerous times; it is possible that the San Vicente bird was the same individual.

Additional Big Bend records indicate that thick-bills nested at Cottonwood Campground, located along the Rio Grande in the southwestern corner of the park, that it had been seen there regularly each summer since 1988, and it nested in 1990 and 1991.

In Arizona, thick-bills have been recorded at least since 1958, the first documented occurrence north of the border. According to *Birds of North America Online*, it "typically occurs along perennial or intermittent streams and rivers with broader floodplains, near riparian woodland edges and clearings with large sycamores and/or cottonwoods." Additional comments about its behavior were included: "The Thick-billed Kingbird makes a big show of each food-capturing flight, quivering the wings and keeping the head feathers erected...with much vocalizing. The species typically builds its nest in inaccessible locations in tall trees."

Currently (July 2019), there is a pair nesting in Portal (Chiricahua Mts.) that have been there for years, according to Bob Behrstock (per. com.). Bob added: "Birds are occasionally reported in canyons in the Santa Ritas and last year or the year before, we had one or two here at Fort Huachuca in Huachuca Canyon. Most of the nesting pairs are along Sonoita Creek near Patagonia (Santa Cruz Co.)."

In Mexico, thick-bills occur primarily along the Pacific Slope from Sonora to Oaxaca. Preferred Mexican habitats, according to Steve Howell and Sophia Webb, in *A Guide to the Birds of Mexico and Northern Central America*, include "Woodland and edge, plantations, semiopen areas with trees, hedges, scrub, etc. mostly in arid to semiarid areas."

I wrote about finding thick-bills along Mexico's Rio Chihuatlán in Jalisco in *Birder's Mexico*:

> We had stopped along the highway to walk along the steam which had once been a beautiful river with a gallery forest, according to Bill Schaldach. We found a ferruginous pygmy-owl, perched on a small acacia, which was being mobbed by a number of birds. The mobbers included social and vermilion flycatchers, a great kiskadee, and a pair of thick-billed kingbirds. The kiskadee and kingbirds were vociferously scolding the pygmy-owl. It eventually flew off into a brushy to hide from its avian persecutors.

Identifying a thick-billed kingbird isn't difficult. It is the only Mexican kingbird with an all-white throat and chest, a blackish-brown cap, and a large, black bill. All the other kingbirds found in Mexico possess a yellow belly. The fork-tailed flycatcher also has a black cap and white undersides, but their tail is much longer.

In addition, the fork-tailed flycatcher is a bird that occurs only along the Gulf in southern Mexico and Guatemala, while thick-bills are found only on the Pacific Slope and are not found so far south as Guatemala.

The presence of thick-billed kingbirds in U.S. has not changed in many years; it pretty well is limited to the few sites mentioned above. Any change in the bird's status in the U.S. will depend upon changes that might be the result of global warming. Droughts that could affect riparian zones would have disastrous impacts upon the well-being of nesting thick-bills.

COUCH'S AND TROPICAL KINGBIRDS

Eight species of Tyrannus kingbirds have been recorded within the United States; all are considered neotropical migrants that nest in the U.S. and overwinter south of the border. Four are widespread in summer: Cassin's, western, and eastern kingbirds, and the scissor-tailed flycatcher. The gray kingbird occurs only in Florida; the fork-tailed and thick-billed kingbirds are only casual vagrants to the United States, although both are known to nest some years. And two are tropical breeders that do occur north of the border: Couch's kingbird is found only in South Texas and the tropical kingbird is known for both South Texas and south-central Arizona.

The Couch's kingbird and the tropical kingbird look pretty much like the majority of the kingbirds: yellow bellies, white throats, short and stout bills, gray to dark gray caps, and black, slightly forked tails. They differ primarily in voice and preferred habitats. The voice of the Couch's kingbird is generally described as a shrill, rolling *breeer*, and a common *kip* note. The call of the tropical kingbird is a rapid, twittering *pip-pip-pip-pip*.

Kent Rylander, in *The Behavior of Texas Birds*, wrote that the call of the Couch's kingbird is "a buzzy chee kweear," while that of the tropical kingbird is a series of "rapid, staccato notes that rise in pitch. Song: a series of high notes (rendered as *pit it it it*) followed by higher trills, usually sung at dawn."

Timothy Brush, in *Nesting Birds of a Tropical frontier*, wrote about their preferred habitats within the Lower Rio Grande Valley, thusly:

> There is a distinct habitat segregation among the three nesting kingbirds, with Couch's being commonest in relatively dense forest areas and scrub, Western being common in agricultural areas and around rural homes and other open inhabited areas, and Tropical Kingbirds more frequent in golf courses, in city parks, and on open campuses of some Valley schools.

I am most familiar with Couch's kingbirds from the years that I worked in Big Bend National Park in West Texas. Although it occurs there only as a casual summer resident and migrant, I included it in *A Field Guide to the Birds of the Big Bend*, thusly:

> Couch's Kingbird. *Tyrannus couchii*. Records extend from an early sighting at Boquillas on April 27, 1966, through the summer and fall months, to an October 9, 1971 sighting at RGV [Rio Grande Village]. During the summer of 1971, I found a lone bird defending a territory and building a nest on a cottonwood at RGV; it remained in the area near the pond behind the store from June 22 through August 4. As far as I could determine, it remained alone but continued to vigorously defend a territory. In the fall, I have recorded Couch's Kingbird on a number of occasions; one of three birds seen at CC [Cottonwood Campground] on September 2, 1968, was collected, and the specimen was later identified as *couchii* [subspecies] by Allan Phillips.

In Mexico, the range of the Couch's kingbird extends southward between the Sierra Madre Oriental and the Gulf to all of the Yucatan Peninsula and to Guatemala and Belize. Preferred habitats, according to Steve Howell and Sophie Webb, in *A Guide to The Birds of Mexico and Northern Central America*, include "Scrubby woodland, forest and edge, plantations, open areas with scattered scrubby woodland of interior, U[uncommon] in arid beach scrub."

My Mexico sightings are varied. I have recorded it on numerus occasions along the Gulf Slope, and I wrote about two of those sightings in *Birder's Mexico*:

> I made a late-afternoon drive toward Matamoros, as far as the cattail pond, and found two more birds of interest. Just east of the cattail pond is a small residence with a couple of mesquite trees in the front yard and a small thornscrub thicket behind the house. A medium-sized hawk was perched on the open mesquite in front of the house, and sat there for several minutes while I identified it as a roadside hawk... And sitting on top of the adjacent mesquite was a Couch's kingbird, a species only recently (1983) considered separate from the tropical kingbird. Couch's kingbird is restricted to eastern Mexico and southeast Texas; I have recorded it as far west as Big Bend National Park.

My second report in *Birder's Mexico* is from Alta Cima, a well-knowing Christmas Bird Count location above Gómez Farías in Tamaulipas:

> Dawn of December 27, 1989 was clear and cold at Alta Cima. Frost had formed overnight on the grass. Birds were evident only by their calls and songs that rang out around the clearing. The loudest and most obvious were those of the spot-breasted wrens; at least four individuals sang from the undergrowth. A blue mockingbird sang briefly, I detected songs of brown-backed solitaires and gray silky-flycatchers up the hillside, and an Altamira oriole contributed to the morning chorus. Then a flock of twenty-five to thirty red-billed pigeons suddenly flew across the clearing.

As the sunlight reached the valley treetops it triggered further activities, and a few additional bird species made themselves known, the most obvious being the social flycatchers…A Couch's kingbird was added to the songfest.

The tropical kingbird, also known by various writers as olive-backed or fork-tailed kingbird, has been recorded in the United States only since the early 1990s. Their numbers rapidly increased so that by early 2000-2004 they were nesting upriver to Laredo. Mark Lockwood and Brush Freeman wrote in *Handbook of Texas Birds* (2004) the following:

> Uncommon and local resident in the Lower Rio Grande Valley. The status of Tropical Kingbird in Texas changed dramatically during the 1990s. Prior to 1991, only a single documented record existed for the state, a specimen collected on 5 December 1909 near Brownsville, Cameron County. Since 1991, this species has become a permanent resident in Cameron and Hidalgo Counties. A few scattered sightings come from father up the Rio Grande in Starr County. Since 1997, Tropical Kingbirds have consistently nesting at Cottonwood Campground in Big Bend National Park, Brewster County.

My primary encounters with the tropical kingbird in the U.S. have occurred in deep South Texas just north of the Lower Rio Grande Valley. I recall my first U.S. sighting along an open area with scattered cotton fields and edged with cane near McAllen. It was alone but seemed rather territorial as it returned again and again to a lone utility pole.

My Mexico records are extensive although I have written about those encounters only once, undoubtedly because the species is so numerous and widespread in Mexico. My one report, in *Birder's Mexico*, was from Chichén Itza in the Yucatan:

> I counted at least sixty black and yellow or gold orioles of five different kinds in the tree. Altamira, orange, orchard, hooded, and yellow-backed orioles were all feeding on the tree's small and inconspicuous greenish-brown flowers…We also identified four kinds of hummers there…Other birds that we recorded in the same tree included both golden-olive and red-vented woodpeckers, tropical kingbird, social and boat-billed flycatchers, blue-gray gnatcatcher, clay-colored robin, rufous-browed peppershrike, four species of warblers, and several yellow-winged tanagers. It was like an avian smorgasbord.

Harry Oberholser, in *The Bird Life of Texas*, wrote that the nesting season of tropical kingbirds extends from "Early or mid-Apr. to late June (eggs, May 5 to June 2) from near sea level to 400 ft." And Brush wrote the following:

> Nests are built in trees or on artificial structures…The Port Isabel nest in 1994 was about 90 feet up, on top of a football stadium light pole. Perhaps the Tropical Kingbird's greater use of golf courses, sports fields, and other habitats with few trees has induced it, like the Western Kingbird, to use artificial structures. In contrast is the Couch's Kingbird, which mainly occurs in denser forest and scrub, where plenty of natural nest sites are available.

Keith Arnold, writing in an article found on the internet, described kingbird nests as "an untidy bowl, apparently built by females but both sexes glean nesting materials in flight. It consists of twigs, strips of bark or Spanish moss, sometimes lined with fine rootlets."

Although tropical kingbird nests are sometimes subjected to parasitism by bronzed cowbirds, Paul Ehrlich and colleagues claim, in The *Birder's Handbook*, that Couch's kingbirds "eject Bronzed Cowbirds eggs from nest."

Like all kingbirds, Couch's and tropical kingbirds are insectivores, actively pursuing flying insects oftentimes for considerable distances and they sometimes circle about like swallows. They occasionally obtain insects on the ground and even on leaves as well. And Brush wrote:

> Tropical kingbirds often make flights of more than 50 feet from a high exposed perch. I have seen them eat mistletoe berries and Chinese tallow fruits in Texas, and they probably consume other fruits, especially in winter…a greater percent of the Valley's Tropical Kingbirds remains in winter, compared with Couch's. Groups of two to five are seen throughout the fall and winter, probably family groups staying together until the following breeding season.

Oberholser also claims that tropical kingbirds

> are one of the few subtropical birds which comes freely in cities and towns. Here it perches on wires, fences, houses, and upper branches of ornamental shrubs and trees…Texas ebony, and others – where it calls, bickers, and makes quick round trips to snap up flying insects. Less solitary than some of the small flycatchers, it gathers, particularly during the nonbeeding season, into large companies…It is generally not shy and may be approached within a reasonable distance.

Kingbirds can, however, be very aggressive toward other birds that invade their territories. Brush wrote that the Couch's kingbird "often is the first species to detect a passing raptor, and it chases raptors and other large birds from its territory. The first indication of an intruding raptor is the repeated *kip* calls with an occasional *breeer* mixed in."

The Couch's kingbird has been well established within Texas for many years and has expended its range west and north in recent years. The tropical kingbird, a more recent arrival also appears to be doing very well. It is very likely that, with changes relative to global warming, that the range of both species may expand northward in time.

GREAT KISKADEE

This is a tropical flycatcher that is found in the United States only in the Lower Rio Grande Valley of Texas. It is one of those "Valley" species that birders travel many miles to see. And what an amazing bird it is! Large for a flycatcher, the great kiskadee is more than nine inches in length, almost twice the size of the Empidonax flycatchers. But its contrasting plumage pattern and vocalizations are what makes this bird so very special.

The great kiskadee is distinctively marked with a russet back and tail, bright yellow chest and belly, and a head pattern with a white collar, wide russet band that runs from the bill through the eyes, and a russet cap. And if that isn't enough, its call is a slow but loud and deliberate *kis-ka-dee*, with emphasis on the *kis* and *dee*. It also gives a loud *kreath* call. Its name is obviously derived from its very distinct *kis-ka-dee* call.

Kent Rylander, in *The Behavior of Texas Birds*, added that its call is a "rapid, staccato, notes that rise in pitch. Song: a series of high notes (rendered as *pit it it*) followed by higher trills, usually sung at dawn."

Although the great kiskadee is found in the United States primarily along the Mexican border in south Texas, its range extends south through Mexico all the way to Argentina. It is most common in the Atlantic and Pacific lowlands; it is not a bird of the tropical highlands.

The majority of my encounters with this flycatcher has principally been in the Lower Rio Grande Valley of Texas. During the many years that I was able to camp at Bentsen-Rio Grande State Park, dawn calls of great kiskadees and plain chachalacas awoke me every morning. Although several other birds, including Altamira orioles and olive sparrows that joined the dawn chorus, kiskadee and chachalaca calls were the loudest. A similar experience was repeated on each camping trip into Mexico. I wrote about the dawn chorus at Rancho Nuevo in *Birder's Mexico*, thusly:

> The loudest of the bird songs was coming from a thicket where a spot-breasted wren repeated its song over and over again…Off to the right was the drawn-out *who whoo* of a red-billed pigeon, and I could hear another a hundred yards ahead to the left. Plain chachalacas, at least four individuals, were also calling somewhere beyond. Two brown jays were screeching in the trees just ahead. An olive sparrow sang from some shrubs a few yards to the left…a ferruginous pygmy-owl added its repetitive single-noted whistle to the chorus. I also detected at least three masked tityras and a golden-fronted woodpecker calling from the same general area. The distinct call of a tufted titmouse, fairly close, was almost overlooked. Further off to the left I detected an elegant trogon…And about three hundred feet ahead, a great kiskadee joined in the dawn chorus.

I also recall a morning along the Rio Cihuatán that runs between the Mexican states of Jalisco and Colima. Once a gallery forest, the streamsides were little more than scattered patches of what was once a significant habitat for a whole array of birds. I wrote about that morning in *Birder's Mexico*:

We found a citreoline trogon in a small patch of trees surprisingly close to the main highway. And we found a ferruginous pygmy-owl perched on a small acacia, and being mobbed by a number of other birds. Included in this party were social and vermilion flycatchers, a pair of thick-billed kingbirds, and a great kiskadee.

All those flycatchers were diving and screaming at the lone pygmy-owl. But I was most impressed by the kiskadee that seemed to dominate the mobbing process. It made dive after dive at the pygmy-owl, even scrapping its back once or twice. Most of the times the pygmy-owl ducked just in time. It finally decided that enough was enough and it made a fast retreat into a nearby brushy area. The kiskadee followed it, screaming at it in kiskadee fashion, until the pygmy-owl was firmly hidden within the brush.

Early mornings in the tropics are like nowhere else. Bird songs are by far the dominant sounds. The dawn chorus may last for as little as twenty minutes or for more than an hour, depending upon the time of year and weather. Some birds sing their territorial song only during this brief period of the day, although they may call or sing other less expressive songs at various other times of day. Most bird songs are different than their calls. To hear the greatest number of bird songs at their peak, one must be out early to experience the dawn chorus.

Tropical naturalist William Beebe provided his impressions of the great kiskadee when he wrote: "The kiskadee has nothing of delicacy or dainty grace. It is beautiful in rufous wings and brilliant yellow under plumage, it is regal with a crown of black, white, and orange...It is the harbinger of the dawn, but so it is an alarm clock."

One of the most extensive discussions of the kiskadee's life history and behavior is by Timothy Brush in *Nesting Birds of a Tropical Frontier;* it includes all of the nesting birds known in the Lower Rio Grande Valley of Texas. Brush wrote that "It is fun to watch Great Kiskadees at any time of year. Whether gleaning fruit in flight, chasing off a grackle or cowbird that comes too close to the nest, or making a shallow dive into the water to capture a fish or aquatic insect, kiskadees are always doing something interesting."

Brush also mentions kiskadee nests: "Nests are large football-shaped domes, usually placed securely in a tree fork or wedged between a transformer and wooden telephone pole. Nests built among smaller branches of the outer canopy sometimes are pulled apart by strong winds, a regular condition in the Valley."

And Rylander stated that nests are "usually buried in dense foliage, a large, bulky structure that is oval or football-shaped, with an entrance on the side. Incubation and parental behavior are poorly known, but both parents vigorously defend the nest against intruders."

I can attest to their vigorous defense of a nest. On finding a kiskadee nest along the entrance road to Santa Ana National Wildlife Refuge, and while trying to photograph that pair of nest-building kiskadees, I was attacked time and again by both birds. I remember being surprised by their loud cries at each dive that continued until I moved elsewhere; one individual even followed me for a hundred feet or more, chastising me for my intrusion.

Later that same day, I returned to the nesting site that was located in a huisache tree overlooking an open pond (see photo 57 above). The birds then seemed more intent in fishing than nest-building. I watched as one member of the pair dove directly into the water from a perch five or six feet above the water, kingfisher-like. On one of six attempts it caught a guppy-sized minnow. It then flew to the same perch, flipped its catch over and swallowed it head-first. I realized that, being a flycatcher, the majority of its food is insects that are caught in mid-air, but tadpoles, freshwater shrimp, and dragonfly nymphs are favorites as well.

Kiskadees also will feed on a variety of larger creatures; small lizards and snakes are examples. Plus, they also will feed on plant materials. I have watched them taking fruit of Turk's-caps at Santa Ana, and I discovered that they also utilize the tiny, extremely hot Chilipiquins. And Brush mentioned that they will "visit feeding stations to eat bread, cooked rice, or bananas, and they even take dog food out of bowls placed on back porches."

Kiskadees utilize a wide variety of sites for nesting. Although most nests are located in various small trees and shrubs, often overlooking water, they also have been reported to nest in cemeteries, alleyways, residential areas, and rural woodlands. And Brush adds a few other locations:

> Strange but evidently safe nesting locations include the superstructure of an electrical substation, the top of a Purple Martin nest box, woodpecker holes, and niches in the façade of a Brazilian church. In tropical banana plantations, the birds wedge their nest in between clusters of fruit. Kiskadees also nest in "ant-acacias" in Mexico and Central America, where the aggressive ants vigorously repel intruders. Wasps often nest in ant-acacias and provide an additional degree of protection.

Although the U.S. range of kiskadees is pretty well limited to the Lower Rio Grande Valley, this species has expanded its range in recent years. It is now considered uncommon in spring, summer and fall in the Del Rio area, and there are numerous sightings as far west as Big Bend National Park. In *Handbook of Texas Birds*, Mark Lockwood and Brush Freemen stated that it nests as far up the coast to Calhoun County; "Kiskadees nested farther up the coast in Baytown, Chambers County, in 2002."

They added that "There are isolated Great Kiskadee records from almost all areas of the state. They have wandered at all seasons, although primarily in spring, as far north as the South Plains and north-central Texas and west to Big Bend National Park, Brewster County, and Imperial Reservoir, Pecos County."

I am convinced that it is only a matter of time, partially due to global warming, that this tough flycatcher will be found throughout the state of Texas, and it may also be recorded in all of the surrounding states.

SULPHUR-BELLIED FLYCATCHER

This is the only flycatcher that breeds in the United States that is heavily streaked above and below. Harry Oberholser described it in *The Bird Life of Texas* as "Heavily streaked with brownish, olive, and buff above, except for rufous rump and tail; blackish gray stroke through eye; white streak over eye and on jaw; whitish throat, speckled finely with blackish; pale yellow below; streaked with blackish gray on breast, sides, and flanks. 7 ½ - 8 ½."

The appearance of a sulphur-bellied flycatcher is truly outstanding; it is almost impossible to misidentify. And its call is also rather unique; it is often described as a loud chatter, like the squeaking of a rubber duck; its song is interpreted as a soft *tre-le-re-re*. Further description of its voice was provided by Steve Howell and Sophie Webb in *A Guide to the Birds of Mexico and Northern Central America*:

> An excited, piercing to shrill 'squeezy-toy'-like *wee'uh* and *weez-ih,* often doubled, may be preceded by short gruff notes, *pek, pek, pek kweez-i-zik kweez-i-zik*, or run into longer series *whee whee whee whee whee-i-eezk'* or *si-chu' w-chee w-chee w-chee w-chee*, etc. Dawn song a bright, slightly slurred phrase followed by a clipped, slightly liquid phrase, *chee-a-leet s-lik* or *chew-ee ti-lit* or *doo-ee ti-u'*, etc., repeated over and over, often before dawn.

The sulphur-bellied flycatcher is a tropical species known in the United States only in southern Arizona and with scattered records in southwest Texas. South of the border, it occurs in Chihuahua, Nuevo León, central Tamaulipas, and southward through Mexico and Central America to Costa Rica. It spends its winter months in Peru and Bolivia.

Its preferred habitats include humid to semiarid forest, edge and clearing, gallery woodlands, and plantations. Its southern Arizona habitat is almost exclusively along riparian corridors with tall trees with high foliage. My earliest sightings occurred during a 1966 visit to Arizona's Santa Rita Mountains south of Tucson. It was one of the southern Arizona specialties that I went there to see.

I also encountered it once at Big Bend National Park in Texas. I wrote about that sightings in *A Field Guide to the Birds of the Big Bend*, thusly:

> Sulphur-bellied Flycatcher. *Myiodynastes luteiventris*. Casual spring migrant, two fall reports. On May 11, 1969, Jim Tucker, Doug Eddleman, and I discovered a lone bird at RGV [Rio Grande Village]; it represented the first known record for Texas. Since then, Glenn Lowe, Jr., reported one at Boulder Meadow on August 5, 1971; Ruth Snyder found one just below Laguna Meadow on May 9, 1976; and A. R. Winshall discovered one on April 15, and Albin Zeitler found it there two days later. The latest report is one found at CC [Cottonwood Campground] on a rainy November 13, 1991, by Sue Weidenfeld.

Sulphur-bellies also have been reported within the Lower Grande Valley in southeast Texas. Timothy Brush included it in *Nesting Birds of a Tropical Frontier* (2005):

> It currently is one of the rarest and most irregular of the nesting flycatchers in Texas. On May 29, 1976, John C. Arvin saw a pair fight with a pair of Golden-fronted Woodpeckers for a nest cavity at Santa Margarita Ranch, Starr County. The flycatchers remained until July 11, but the dead tree containing the cavity was felled by a violent thunderstorm on June 3. The pair returned for two more breeding seasons (McKinney 2002).

Sulphur-bellies are one of the latest neotropical migrants to arrive on their U.S. nesting grounds; they are considered a long-distant migrant that spend their winters in the eastern Andean foothills of Columbia and Ecuador.

In Mexico, I have encountered this fascinating flycatcher on several occasions, but I wrote about those sightings, in *Birder's Mexico*, on only three occasions. The earliest was along the Río Corona, considered the northeastern edge of its breeding range. Besides sulphur-bellies that day, I also recorded bronze-winged and lineated woodpeckers, Mexican crow, spot-breasted wren, clay-colored robin, crimson-collared grosbeak, and blue bunting in the same location.

Later, in the interior highlands, while searching for tufted jays in the Sierra Madre above Mazatlán, I discovered a ferruginous pygmy-owl being mobbed by several songbirds. I wrote the following:

> The most aggressive of the avian mobbers had been one of the smallest, the golden vireo. A pair of these birds had soundly scolded the pygmy-owl from the nearby oak foliage, and remained there in defiance until the owl departed. A lone sulphur-bellied flycatcher seemed to be bravest and actually flew close enough to make the owl, which is just about the same size as the flycatcher, duck its head with each pass.

My third report was from Paval, a camping site along the trail to El Triunfo in the extreme southeastern corner of Mexico, just above the Guatemalan border. The following morning was spent birding the surroundings before continuing our hike higher into the mountains. Key birds found at dusk included the pauraque, mottled owl, striped cuckoo, Prevost's ground-sparrow, tody motmot, long-tailed manakin, and an emerald-chinned hummingbird feeding on some red *Salvia* bushes. And I added a number of flycatchers to my list: "paltry tyrannulet, yellow-bellied elaenia, common tody-flycatcher, eye-ringed flatbill; royal, boat-billed, social, brown-capped, and sulphur-bellied flycatchers; a yellow-olive flycatcher was constructing a round pendant nest of black moss."

The sulphur-bellied flycatcher is one of only six North American flycatchers that is a cavity nester. More than two dozen flycatcher species build a cup nest on a tree or shrub; two build a globular mass nest. Sulphur-bellies utilized cavities constructed by woodpeckers, usually 25 to 45 feet above the ground. Paul Ehrlich and colleagues provide details about their courtship and nesting in *The Birder's Handbook*:

> Displays: Male and female vigorously shake heads, snap their beaks, and duet. Pair then fly closely following each other, occ perch together, all within

a small area. Nest: Usu in cavity of sycamore, nest usu built almost to level of opening, bulky, oft on base of twigs and sticks, cup of decid leaf petioles, pine needles, without soft lining. Perennial...Begins nesting later than most other birds in its range. Not as aggressive as kingbirds, but will persistently defend nest. Male does not feed incubating female. Young [3 or 4] hatch synchronously.

Sulphur-bellies may compete for nesting cavities with other hole-nesting birds, even elegant trogons. Both parents feed the nestlings that begin flight at 16 to 18 days of age.

Sulphur-bellies' diet consists primarily of insects that they take by aerial pursuits or by gleaning leaves and branches. They forage by watching for prey from a perch, then flying out to capture insects; they may hover in their pursuit. They also utilize fruit in season.

The sulphur-bellied flycatcher faces various threats: local impacts on riparian zones from overgrazing and wood-cutters, and global warming that may severely lower rainfall necessary to maintain essential habitats.

GREATER PEWEE

Arizona's Chiricahua National Park supports several reasonably common Mexican songbirds. Although none is as abundant as the Mexican jay, others include the heavily-streaked sulphur-bellied flycatcher, with its yellowish underparts and rusty tail, Mexican chickadee, with a coal-black cap and bib and dark gray flanks, and the active bridled titmouse, with a tall crest and black-and-white head. Also common are the red-faced warbler, with its red face and throat, and cap black; the painted redstart, all black except for a bright red belly and snow-white wing patches and outer tail feathers; the yellow-eyed junco, with its rufous back and wing coverts, black tail with white outer feathers, and gray head with bright yellow eyes offset by black lores. Less common birds of Mexican affinity include the whiskered screech-owl, blue-throated and magnificent hummingbirds, Arizona woodpecker, greater pewee, dusky-capped flycatcher, and olive warbler.

The greater pewee, earlier known as Coue's flycatcher, is a rather stately bird with overall brown plumage. Breeding birds possess pale underparts and a dark head with a short crest and a bill with a yellow-orange lower mandible. Its back is dark gray-brown with two yellowish wing-bars. And its voice, especially its Jose Maria song, is truly unique. Steve Howell and Sophie Webb, in *A Guide to the Birds of Mexico and Northern Central America*, described its' voice as follows:

A sharp to mellow *beek beek beek* or *puip-puip-puip*, at time repeated steadily, much like Olive-sided Flycatcher. Song a bright to slightly plaintive *wheee* to *whee-wheu* (or *Jo-sé Ma-ría*), varied to *whee'tee-tee whee-wee'* or *wheeu tew tee di-irit* or *chewdl-it*, in full song, this last phrase may also be repeated over and over.

This large flycatcher can be fairly common in pine-oak woodlands in the southern mountains of Arizona, and in Mexico; its habitat preferences include pine-oak, evergreen, and semi-deciduous forest and edge, and clearings. Further south it inhabits forested slopes in both the Sierra Madre Occidental and Sierra Madre Oriental, and extending to El Salvador and Nicaragua.

Harry Oberholser provided additional comments on its life history in *The Bird Life of Texas*:

> The bird breeds in pine-oak situations in canyons, on slopes and ridges, and in timber along streams where it saddles a moss and lichen up moderately high (15 to 25 feet) on a limb of a conifer or deciduous tree. The territory of a nesting pair is of considerable size and is carefully defended. Coues' is not gregarious, but during migration and in winter it sometimes associates with companies of nuthatches, warblers, tanagers, and other small forest roaming species.

In Mexico, I have recorded greater pewees on several occasions. I wrote about one of those sightings in the Sierra Autlán in *Birder's Mexico*, thusly:

> On May 1, we arrived at La Cumbre at 5:00 A.M., and immediately hiked up the trail into the humid pine-oak forest habitat. Eared poorwills called along the lower parts of the route until 5:35 A.M. At least three Colima warblers were singing in the canyon below the trail. The sweet calls of Hutton's vireos were prominent sounds from the oaks. The canyon wren-like call of ivory-billed woodcreeper was heard several times. And further up the ridge the dominant calls were the ho-say Marie of the greater pewees.

Besides Arizona, the greater pewee has also been reported in the Texas Big Bend Country. I included it in *A Field Guide to the Birds of the Big Bend*:

> Greater Pewee. *Contopus pertinax*. Casual spring and fall visitor; winter records. Spring reports, all from the high Chisos Mountains, extend from an April 26, 1984 sighting at Boot Canyon by Anne and Jim Bellamy, to a June 8, 1968, observation of a singing bird on Emory Peak above Laguna Meadow (Wauer). Fall reports range from mid-August to mid-September; one on September 3, 1973; Bonnie McKinney found one there on September

12, 1983, and Charles and Louise Gambill recorded it on September 2, 1983. The two winter records, both from CC [Cottonwood Campground], include one by Jerry and Nancy Strickland on December 21, 1974, and William and Alice Roe reported one, perhaps the same bird, there on January 6, 1975.

Finally, I recorded a lone greater pewee in Pine Canyon on April 29, 1999.

NORTHERN BEARDLESS-TYRANNULET

This little flycatcher is unique in several ways. Its tiny size, its plain appearance, and its habitat preference give it almost a ghost-like character. Its plumage is grayish-olive overall with a brown cap and blackish wings with two pale whitish wing bars, and a white throat. A careful look also will reveal a slight crest. And its common name was derived from its lack of bristles around its tiny bill that help other small birds capture insects.

Harry Oberholser, in *The Bird Life of Texas*, provides an additional description: "*Camptostoma imberbe* of A.O.U. check-list, 1957. A tiny, very plain flycatcher with a short, dark, "Roman nose" (lower mandible lighter in color) and small head; olive gray above; whitish below; indistinct eye-ring; buffy wing-bars. Length, 4 ½ in.; wingspan, 7 in."

Its voice also is rather distinct, an innocuous, descending series of clear *peer* or *pee-yerp* notes. Kent Rylander, in *The Behavior of Texas Birds*, described its call as a "loud and repetitive piping, rendered as *pee yeerp*, possibly the best field mark since in appearance this species closely resembles an immature Verdin (found in the same habitat). The thin, high song consists of three to five descending *eees*."

Timothy Brush also wrote about a "dawn song" in *Nesting Birds of a Tropical Frontier*:

> Dawn songs are a feature of the territorial behavior of many flycatchers, including the tyrannulet. The male perches high up in an open location and gives its emphatic dawn song from the first light until perhaps half an hour after sunrise. This song is not given at other times of day, and tyrannulets seem particularly quiet toward dusk, at a time when other species may be singing. In cases where I knew the nesting location, the dawn song might be given more than 300 feet from the nest, and when the male usually approached the nest tree and gradually switched over to the normal song (the *pier* series) as the day brightened.

The tyrannulet is another tropical species; its range barely extends into the United States in deep south Texas and southeastern Arizona. U.S. birds usually spend their winter months south of the border from southern Sonora, central Nuevo León, and southern Tamaulipas. Its Texas range was described by Mark Lockwood and Brush Freeman, in *Handbook of Texas Birds*, thusly:

> Rare to locally uncommon resident in the Lower Rio Grande Valley, northward through the Central Sand Plain, Northern Beardless-Tyrannulet appears to be increasing in abundance in the Lower Rio Grande Valley. There is single report further north of one in Goliad County...There have been two unexpected

records from Presidio County in the Trans-Pecos, one at a remote spring in the foothills of the Chinati Mountains...and another observed near Ruidoso.

In southern Arizona it occurs in dense scrub areas usually near water, such as along Sonoita Creek and the San Pedro and Santa Cruz Rivers. It usually moves south during the winter months, but it increasingly has been found to remain in winter.

The majority of my encounters with tyrannulets occurred during the three years (1990-1992) that I spent surveying the birdlife on the Noria Division of the King Ranch in southeast Texas. Although I principally was involved with population surveys of the ferruginous pygmy-owl, I recorded all the birds observed on each trip.

I found that tyrannulets never were common; the following are seven examples: During a two-day survey on November 2 and 3, 1989, I recorded 2039 birds of 95 species and only one tyrannulet. A three-day survey from December 5 to 7, 1989, I recorded 2114 birds of 83 bird species and a single tyrannulet. From March 17 to 20, 1990, I recorded 1295 birds of 89 species and three tyrannulets. From August 27 through 29, 1990, I recorded 1026 birds of 102 species, but only one tyrannulet. On January 2 and 3, 1991, I recorded 989 bird of 70 species and one tyrannulet. On October 10 and 11, 1991, I recorded 1135 birds of 75 species and not a single tyrannulet. And on March 22 to 25, 1992, I recorded 986 birds of 118 species and five tyrannulets.

Nests are round, baseball-size, similar to that of a verdin, with an entrance near the top. They usually are hidden in clumps of leaves or mistletoe and constructed of grasses and weeds. Harry Oberholser added that their nests occur

> In flat, sandy lowlands, edges of groves, or scattered trees; in bush or tree, usually near ground...composed of palm fibers, weed stems, or other vegetable materials; lined with cottonlike and weed fibers. Eggs: 2, white; spotted with dark brown, reddish brown, and lilac, markings sometimes forming ring about larger end.

And in *The Birder's Handbook*, Paul Ehrlich and colleagues claim that nests can occur on tree limb from four to fifty feet above ground, and their diet is "mostly insects; few berries and seeds…In winter, reportedly forages mostly by gleaning from bark of twigs."

Bush provides us with a glimpse of this tiny bird's personality:

> Tyrannulets, as the name implies, can be aggressive when defending their nest tree. I have seen one chase a foraging Ladder-backed Woodpecker or Tufted Titmouse that got too close to an active nest. However, since titmice often poke their heads into various crevices, clumps of ball-moss, or even nests, they could be a threat to eggs or nestlings. Tyrannulets sometimes briefly chase Orange-crowned Warblers in mixed-species flocks.

And Harry Oberholser wrote that it behaves like a flycatcher:

> This usually inconspicuous bird perches on the top branch of tree from where it makes short aerial sorties after flying insects. However, during much of the year it also inspects lower branches of trees and bushes in the manner of a vireo; here it gleans scale insects, caterpillars, butterfly larvae, ants, and occasionally small berries and seeds.

The long-term status of this little flycatcher depends primarily on the stability of the mesquite and other arid woodlands. It is unlikely that these environments will change in the near future. And with global warming, their essential habitats are likely to increase.

MEXICAN JAY

I must admit that, in spite of the colorful aspects of green jays, I am partial to Mexican jays. Probably that is because of the amount of time I have spent with this bird within its natural haunts in the Chisos Mountains of Texas and in Mexico's Maderas del Carmen in the state of Coahuila. I wrote about one Mexican jay encountered in Big Bend in *For All Seasons, A Big Bend Journal*:

> March 9 (1969). Today's hike to Boot Spring produced a total of thirty-four bird species, none of which were migrants. Although a few early northbound migrants are beginning to appear in the lowlands, especially along the Rio Grande, evidently none of the early migrants are passing through the highlands. However, several of the permanent resident birds were already in their breeding cycle. The common Mexican jays were nest-building. Although they were reasonably quiet (for jays), I observed two separate pairs carrying nesting materials. At Laguna Meadow, I watched one of these attractive, all-blue birds gathering horse hairs from along the trail. They utilize this hair as a lining in their twig-and-grass nests. It apparently gives the nest lining a soft, mattress-like texture.

Paul Ehrlich and colleagues discussed nesting Mexican jays in *The Birder's Handbook*. They wrote that during courtship, the male "circles females with his wings and tail tilted toward her; aligns himself sideways to female, oft reversing direction through 180 degrees jump." They added that nesting birds use a "horizontal limb or crotch of oak tree, occ. conif.; conspicuous and bulky with platform of twigs supporting cup of rootlets lined with fine grass and hair. No mud." The eggs are pale green marked with green.

They also pointed out that Mexican jays are communal breeders in that "more than one bird will provide care in rearing the young from one nest... Cooperative breeders may exhibit shared maternity, shared paternity, or both."

Nest assistance for the monogamous pair is often provided by several individuals within the flock. Last year's youngsters often are "helpers" with the nest and nestlings, all non-sexual activities.

The diet of Mexican jays consists primarily of acorns, although they will take advantage of various other goodies that come their way. The acorns are broken open so they can obtain the soft inside material by heavy beats from the jay's strong bill. And birds that reside near camp sites learn very quickly to take advantage of human scraps.

Like all members of the Corvidae Family, considered the "brainiest" of all the bird families, they are opportunists. They will steal food from other birds, they will cache extra food for later use, and they will search cache sites of other birds for what can be recovered. They may then re-cache the food, usually in a place that others are unable to find it.

I included a general discussion of this bird in my *A Field Guide to the Birds of the Big Bend*. I wrote:

> Mexican Jay...Common permanent resident. This jay was known as Gray-breasted Jay for several years until its earlier name was restored by the AOU [American Ornithologist Union] (according to Van Remsen). It is one of the most conspicuous birds of the Chisos Mountains, where flocks of five to 18 individuals are commonplace. CBC [Christmas Bird Counts] participants tallied 25 in 1966, 222 in 1967, 180 in 1969, and 106 in 1970. Nesting occurs during April, May, and June. I found nests on Grave's oak near Laguna Meadow on May 8, 1970, and on an Emory oak near the Window on May 11, 1968. Anne Bellamy found a nest she referred to as a "large arrangement of disarranged small sticks," at Boot Springs on May 29, 1983; and C. Phillip Allen reported fledged birds at Boot Springs on June 1, 1963. There apparently is some movement to lower elevations during some winters. I found one in upper Big Brushy Canyon, in the northern part of the Dead Horse Mountains, on October 13, 1969, and another at RGV [Rio Grande Village] on December 13, 1969.

During any hike into the Chisos Mountains, it is rare when one cannot hear the call notes of Mexican jays. And at any of the camp sites one is likely to be greeted by one or several of these vociferous birds. I have spent considerable time sitting outside the cabin at Boot Spring watching these fascinating birds. If they are not given a handout very soon, they are likely to sail away to some other jay business. But often, before departing, they will hop around the open area to check for possible people scraps. Then they may simply fly up to one of the adjacent pines and loudly proclaim their frustration. A typical call is a ringing *wink* or a series of *wink* notes. Herbert Brandt, in *Texas Bird Adventures*, wrote that the Mexican jay calls in the Chisos Mountains were best written as *'oint-oint-oint.'* He added that the notes were "delivered more slowly, and evenly, in a high pitch," in comparing those with the Arizona Mexican jay.

Herbert Brandt's book on his adventures in the Chisos Mountains was one of the books that I read before moving to Big Bend National Park as Chief Park Naturalist in 1966. I thoroughly absorbed that book. And after moving there I was eager to visit all of the locations mentioned. I hiked to Boot Springs and the South Rim on numerous occasions and I learned to appreciate Brandt's *Texas Bird Adventures* even more.

GREEN JAY

Green jays are tropical birds, reaching the United States only in extreme southern Texas. So, finding several of these colorful birds in my yard in Victoria, Texas, more than 200 miles north of the Texas-Mexico border, was a real shocker! And these birds remained in the area for several weeks; they were even included in the 2005 Christmas Bird Count. I found nine individuals in three separate flocks on the Mission Valley Count, including at least five in my yard. And at least nine individuals in three flocks were found on the nearby Guadalupe Delta Count. My yard birds remained for about three weeks and then departed. I have no idea why they first appeared so far north of their normal ranges or why they then departed and where they went. Probably, they returned to South Texas and their normal range.

It is not unusual for birds to wander after nesting, sometimes for great distances. Even buff-bellied hummingbirds, one of the resident hummers in the Victoria area, can often be found further north into Louisiana in fall. Most birds, however, normally retreat southward for winter. This is likely to occur for green jays as well, but their December-January appearance in the Victoria area was not part of a normal post-nesting dispersal.

One reason for some bird's northward movement may relate to changes in essential habitat that could be related to either climate change or habitat destruction. It is pretty well accepted that some of the more mobile critters, including many birds, can gradually move into acceptable habitats and leave habitats that are no longer acceptable behind. The behavior of some species moving into new areas may, in a sense, be exploring new areas. Locating new acceptable habitats eventually may prove useful if it becomes necessary to expand their range.

Green jays can hardly be misidentified; they are one of a kind. They possess a green mantle and wings, a dark green tail, a greenish-yellow belly, and the underside of the tail is bright yellow. But it is their head that is so spectacular. It includes a bright purple-blue nape and a black throat and eye-patch that is divided by a purple patch. They truly are beautiful birds!

Because of their almost gaudy colors, green jays have been a favorite of bird photographers and painters. John O'Neill's painting of two green jays in a flowering huisache shrub, included in *John P. O'Neill Great Texas Birds*, is a favorite. John Arvin wrote comments that accompany the painting, as follow:

> Like most jays, Green Jays are highly social creatures. After the breeding season, the birds form bands of four to ten individuals and roam widely. These are probably family groups, perhaps composed of a pair of breeding adults and their offspring from the last breeding season or two. It is the wandering group of Green Jays that finds suitable habitat may well settle and remain to breed the following season.

Green jays are extremely gregarious birds that are usually found in flocks and often are heard before they are seen. Their call is a raspy series of *cheh-cheh-cheh* notes. Timothy Brush, in *Tropical Birds of the Tropical Frontier*, mentions that their "scolding call is an intensification of the normal *eh-eh-eh-eh* calls used in jay interactions." Brush adds, "Often a snake, bobcat, or owl is the object of the jays' loud attention, but they may also give the same calls during territorial conflicts." Another noted green jay call sounds like an alarm bell.

Kent Rylander, in *The Behavior of Texas Birds*, described it's call as "a rapid, energetic *chick chick chick*, or slower *cleep cleep cleep*, as well as a rattle that has been compared to the sound of a cricket frog. These and other calls are heard year-round."

Of course, all jays are noisy. There are nine resident species in North America – blue, gray, Steller's, Mexican, and pinyon jays, and Florida, island, and Western scrub-jays – and all of them are well-known loud-mouths. In fact, the *jay, jay, jay* calls of the widespread blue jay are where their name was originally derived. But perhaps the 11-inch-long green jay is the most vocal of them all.

Green jays are one of the Texas specialty birds, found nowhere else in the United States. I remember that I traveled all the way from Big Bend National Park, where I was working at the time, to the Lower Rio Grande Valley just to see one of these and a few other specialty birds. And yet, several years later after retiring from the National Park Service and moving to Victoria, they showed up in my yard. I had installed several bird feeders, both seed and hummingbird feeders, and the green jays found one of the platform feeders to their liking. I had placed a few orange pieces on that feeder, a favorite green jay handout.

During earlier years, when anyone wanting to see green jays in the U.S., they were required to visit the Lower Rio Grande Valley. Since then they have been found in a much broader region of South Texas. Mark Lockwood and Brush Freeman provided an excellent perspective on the green jay's overall status in Texas in their *Handbook of Texas Birds* (2004). They wrote:

> Common to uncommon resident from the Lower Rio Grande Valley north to Live Oak, Bee, and southern Maverick Counties. Green Jays have been found with increasing regularity during the winter north of the breeding range to southern Val Verde, Kinney, and Uvalde Counties. These winter incursions may be the prelude to a range expansion northward. Wandering individuals have been reported just north of the normal range to Bexar, Victoria, and Calhoun Counties, while vagrants have been found in Brazos, Johnson, and Midland Counties.

The green jay's nesting season occurs from March to mid-July, during which time they are less gregarious than they are during most of the year. Courtship was described by Rylander: "The female bobs a few times, and the male responds by assuming a sleek posture; this display is followed by mutual bill caressing."

Nests usually are constructed in thorny shrubs and in low trees, always below 20 feet from the ground. The nests are bulky cup-shaped structures of thorny twigs and small stems, and usually are lined with bits of moss, dry grasses, and leaves. The female lays three to five eggs in the cup-shaped structure. She does the majority of the incubation, but both adults feed the nestlings. Fledging occurs in 14 to 16 days.

Nesting green jays do suffer brood parasitism from bronzed cowbirds, and they rarely are captured by predators such as sharp-shinned and Cooper's hawks in the U.S. and by bat falcons and forest-falcons in the tropics.

The green jay diet consists primarily of seeds, especially acorns and ebony seeds, as well as insects, spiders and other arthropods, although they also will utilize various human handouts. When food is plentiful, they will cache extra food for a later time. And to demonstrate their smarts, they have been recorded utilizing a stick as a tool to extract insects from tree bark. Also, these jays are extremely inquisitive. They are the first to alert others of a predator, and they seem alert to any changes in their territory.

They normally do not stray far from their prime habitats in riparian and thornscrub areas. It seems that, even when feeding in the open, they are never far from heavy vegetation where they can readily retreat if threatened. And more often than not, they remain in small flocks. Brush stated: "Green Jays maintain group territories, in which young from the previous breeding season remain with their parents. These immature birds do not breed or bring food to their parents' next set of offspring, but they do help defend the territory against other Green Jay groups."

And Harry Oberholser, in *The Bird Life of Texas*, wrote that the green jay is "skillful at keeping itself concealed when stalked, but if the stalker turns to walk away, several birds are quite likely to set up an outcry; some may even come to the edge of the brush to look the intruder over."

Jays are members of the Corvidae Family, considered the "brainiest" of all the bird families. They are opportunists and will steal food from other birds, and they will cache extra food for later use. Plus, they will search cache sites of other birds for what can be recovered. They may then re-cache the food, usually in a place that others are unable to find it.

The long-term survival of green jay populations in the U.S. is of special interest. Global warming is likely to lead to range creep northward. It is unlikely that the species will ever decline to any extent. In Mexico, this bird is so common and widespread that any decline is doubtful. They seem to be doing very well throughout their range.

AUDUBON'S ORIOLE

There are two orioles that occur in the Lower Rio Grande region of Texas, and are not found elsewhere in the United States: Altamira and Audubon's Orioles. Both are gorgeous birds but noticeably different in appearance. Altamira oriole is orange and black while Audubon's oriole is yellow and black. They also utilize very different habitats. Altamira orioles generally occur within riparian areas, while Audubon's orioles, also known as black-headed orioles, prefer more arid habitats to the north of the Rio Grande, namely the yucca grassland and Tamaulipas scrub habitats.

Audubon's orioles, earlier known as black-headed orioles, possess an all-black head and throat, greenish back, black wings with whitish wing bars, yellow undersides, and a black tail. Their bill is black above and silvery below.

The voice of the Audubon's oriole is rather distinct. It was described by Steve Howell and Sophie Webb, in *A Guide to the Birds of Mexico and Northern Central America*, as "a nasal *yehnk*, often doubled and repeated, and a clear *peu* and *hew-hoo*, the 2nd note higher. And a sad, rich, often hesitant series of whistles, rising and falling, often with nasal calls thrown in."

And Kent Rylander described its voice in *The Behavior of Texas Birds,* thusly: "Call a harsh *ike ike ike*, similar to the Altamira Oriole's call note, but higher pitched. Song: several slow, sweet, melancholy whistles, each on a different pitch, like a young boy idly whistling. It is sometimes rendered as *peut pou it*. This species is much less vocal than the Altamira Oriole."

Harry Oberholser mentioned its flight and diet in *The Bird Life of Texas*, as "strong [flight] but seldom much prolonged. Birds forage quietly in trees and bushes, taking mostly insects (beetles, moths, others), but also small fruits, such as hackberries and mesquite beans." Oberholser also compared Audubon's orioles with green jays:

> In short, this oriole, like the Green Jay, spends much of its time hiding behind thick cover of leaves; both species tend to choose the tallest and densest trees in the landscape. The Black-headed [Audubon's] is able to inhabit somewhat lower brush than does the Green Jay; apparently, this is why it is rather more likely to be found north of the Rio Grande delta. It seems to be a rather sedentary bird and is frequently found in pairs throughout the year.

The range of Audubon's orioles in the United States is pretty well limited to South Texas, within the Tamaulipan scrub zone that extends from below Laredo eastward to near the Gulf and north to an area west of Corpus Christi. In Mexico, their range occurs in two regions, south of South Texas to southern Veracruz and along the Pacific Slope from Jalisco to Oaxaca.

Audubon's orioles build their short, basket-nests on yuccas and various thorny shrubs. The nest is a small hanging pouch that usually is five to fifteen feet above the ground. It is woven from grasses, primarily from fresh green grasses. Timothy Brush described nest locations in *Nesting Birds of a Tropical Frontier*: "Nests are usually well hidden in dense foliage of trees such as mesquite or Texas persimmon or in epiphytic *Tillandsia* in cedar elms or hackberries. Audubon's Orioles are apparently not inclined to nest near other species as other orioles are, thus they tend to nest solitarily."

I got to know Audubon's orioles reasonably well during the years that I conducted breeding bird surveys in South Texas. Their somewhat mournful songs provided easy early morning tallies. Although I only actually observed maybe a third of the number counted, their songs were readily identified.

Oberholser also wrote about the history of Audubon's orioles within the United States:

> Beginning in the 1920s, the mesquite and ebony woodlands of the Rio Grande
> delta have been increasingly cleared to make room for citrus, cotton, grain,

vegetables, and livestock. This clearing greatly reduced the habitat of all woodland birds. Furthermore, the opening up of the country and introduction of cattle increased the cowbird population. Black-headed [Audubon's] Orioles are frequent victims of cowbirds, especially of the Red-eyed Bronzed form. *Icterus graduacaudus* still occupies most of its old range in the United States (meaning south Texas), but its density since the 1920s has been low. By the 1960s, its population was so thin that an Audubon Christmas Bird Count of four individuals in any locality was usually sufficient to ensure a high count for the nation.

ALTAMIRA ORIOLE

The Altamira oriole is one of the specialty birds of the Lower Rio Grande Valley in south Texas, an area popular to hundreds of birders year-round. Altamiras are not found elsewhere in the U.S., but they are easily located in the Valley. Firstly, because they are very vocal, and their songs, a series of clear whistle notes, are commonplace. The song has been described as a disjointed series of whistles and other sounds, some flutelike in quality.

Kent Rylander described its voice in *The Behavior of Texas Birds*:

Call: a harsh, fussing *ike ike ike*, often the best indicator of their presence, as they typically stay hidden in foliage. Song: a disjointed series of whistles and other sounds, some flutelike in quality. It has been compared to the Baltimore Oriole's song. Both males and females are very vocal, and the loud song carries a considerable distance.

And secondly is that their long pendulant nests (two feet or more) are readily apparent. Only the female builds the nest, while the male waits and preens nearby, keeping watch for intruders. Or he may follow his mate while she gathers nesting material, such as grasses to striped pieces of yucca to almost anything that can be woven into a strong basket. Nests usually are suspended from flexible, slender terminal branches, at least 16 feet high, over open space.

The Altamira oriole is one of the yellow-orange and black orioles. Adults possess bright yellow underparts, except for a black throat, reddish-orange head, black bill and lores, and a black back and wings with a single white wing bar and streaks, and a black tail. Some adult males show an almost reddish forehead. It is a striking bird!

This oriole is primarily a Mexican species with a range that barely reaches the United States, and its southern range extends southward along the Gulf Coast, all of the Yucatan Peninsula, and into northern South America. In fact, its name was derived from Altamira, a city and area in southern Tamaulipas, where it was first collected. It also occurs along the southern Pacific Slope to Central America and Nicaragua.

In the United States, Altamira orioles only occur in extreme south Texas, along the Rio Grande, upriver only to Zapata County; it very rarely strays northward to Kleberg County. Mark Lockwood and Brush Freeman adds, in *Handbook of Texas Birds*, that "Altamira Oriole was first documented in Texas in 1938 and was seen infrequently through the 1950s. The first documented nesting record did not come until 1951." They added that the "species underwent an impressive population growth beginning in the early 1960s. Some observers suspect, however, that Altamira Oriole numbers in Texas are now declining."

In the U.S., this bird is found primarily in the riparian habitats, such as that along the lower Rio Grande, but in the tropics, its habitat preference consists of "humid to semi-humid woodland, forest edge, gardens, and hedges," according to Steve Howell and Sophie Webb, in *A Guide to the Birds of Mexico and Northern Central America*. They also mention that they often occur "in large flocks during migration (mainly Sep. and Apr.), in winter often in mixed-species flocks."

I certainly can attest to mixed wintertime flocks. Writing in *Birder's Mexico*, about birding the Yucatan at Chichén Itza, I included the following:

I counted at least sixty black and yellow or gold orioles of five different kinds in the tree. Altamira, orange, orchard, hooded, and yellow-backed orioles were all feeding on the tree's small and inconspicuous greenish-brown flowers. Individuals and groups of three or four orioles came and went during the thirty or forty minutes that we watched the flowering kapok tree.

BLACK-VENTED ORIOLE

A single adult female black-vented oriole was sporadically seen at Rio Grande Village, in Big Bend National Park, between September 1968 and October 1970. It was first discovered on the morning of September 27, 1968; I watched it for several minutes among the foliage of a thicket along the nature trail. Later in the day I identified it from reading descriptions by Emmet Blake (1953) and George M. Sutton (1951), but I could not find it the following morning or on several following visits to the area.

On April 25, 1969, I again saw an adult black-vented oriole (*Icterus wagleri*) less than 300 feet from the location of the first sighting. For more than 40 minutes I watched it and six other orioles (an adult female and immature hooded oriole, and two females, one adult, and one immature male orchard orioles) chase each other from tree to tree within the campground. The black-vented oriole appeared to be in close association with the immature male hooded oriole.

On May 1, as I was again observing *I. wagleri* at the same location (with presumedly, the same six orioles), I met Ty and Julia Hotchkiss, who were camped at RGV. When I informed them of the bird's identity, they graciously offered to photograph the bird for further documentation. During the following three weeks, they took more than 50 feet of 16 mm movie film and eight color slides. *I. wagleri* was further verified by several additional birders.

These sightings represent the first authenticated records of the black-vented oriole for the United States, although there is a questionable sighting by Herbert Brown from the Patagonia Mountains of Arizona in 1910. South of the border, it occurs from Sonora, Chihuahua, and Nuevo Leon, south through Guatemala and Honduras to El Salvador (in winter) and northern Nicaragua. The nearest Mexican records of breeding black-vents to Big Bend are approximately 350 miles to the south, about 15 miles below Goméz Farías, Coahuila.

By mid-May, it was evident that the black-vented oriole at Rio Grande Village was not nesting, and that it was not paired. Its behavior gave no indication that it was defending a territory. Yet by midmorning it would usually disappear into the dense floodplain vegetation and often would not return to the campground portion of its range until late afternoon or evening. By 6:30 a.m. the next day it was back in the campground with many immature orchard orioles or the one or two immature hooded orioles that still were present. All these birds seemed to prefer the fruits of the squaw bush, which was ripening throughout May and June. And on May 1989, I watched *I. wagleri* feed on flowers of desert willow for several minutes, and on June 28 it caught a cicada, tore the wings off, and consumed the softer parts of the body, dropping the rest to the ground.

In order to obtain close-up photographs for racial identification, as well as to band the bird so that it could be recognized it if it returned again, I made several attempts to net it between June 28 and July 4. On July 1, I placed a mounted great horned owl, a species that occurs commonly in the immediate vicinity, on the ground next to the mist net. The black-vented oriole perch ten feet above the stuffed bird and watched while a pair of mockingbirds launched attack after attach on the owl until both were caught in the netting. I even drew a black-vented oriole on cardboard, colored it with the proper colors, and mounted the drawing on a stick next to the net. This, too, was a failure – *I. wagleri's* only reaction was one of vague curiosity.

Yet it did show interest in people on a number of occasions. Several times I observed it watching campers going about their routine duties, and on one occasion it flew into a tree above two children who were rolling a red rubber ball around on the ground. It sat there watching this activity for about four minutes before flying off to another perch. On only two occasions did I observe it showing any aggression toward another oriole.

Finally, by moving the nets each time *I. wagleri* changed position, I succeeded in capturing it on July 4. Closer examination showed that it was in nonbreeding status; it clearly lacked evidence of a brood patch and had no cloacal protuberance. Close examination of the bill and cere also showed no indication that the bird had been caged at any time. Close-up photographs of the chest were sent to Allan Phillips, who identified the bird racially as the *wagleri* form of eastern Mexico. The chest had a light chestnut tinge.

After carefully photographing the major features of the bird, I placed a band (no. 632-25253) on its right leg and released it. It immediately flew south to the floodplain portion of its territory, dove into the dense vegetation, and was not seen the rest of the day. By July 10, however, it was right back to the same habits and allowed good binocular examination for the first half of the morning.

In early August, it became quite shy and had to be searched for among the dense foliage along the nature trail. I last saw it that year on September 19, exactly one year after the original date of discovery. In 1970, I found it again in the same locality from April 17 through September 21 and again on October 10. A good number of birders observed the same banded bird throughout the summer, but it has not been reported since.

Juncos are one of the most widespread of all the birds in North America, from Alaska to northern Mexico. There are two species of juncos, the dark-eyed junco, *Junco hyemalis*, and the yellow-eyed junco, *Junco phaeonotus*. The yellow-eyed junco is a tropical bird that reaches the United States as a breeding species only in southeastern Arizona and southwestern New Mexico, although it also is a casual visitor to Big Bend National Park in south Texas.

Dark-eyed juncos are divided into five forms or subspecies, although adjacent populations do interbreed on occasions. The common eastern bird, known as the slate-colored junco, occurs from the Atlantic Coast eastward to near the Mississippi River. The Oregon junco is a widespread species of the West Coast that can be found eastward into the Rocky Mountains. Pink-sided birds, probably a form of Oregon juncos, are scattered from Oregon into the Southwest. The more common gray-headed juncos occur through much of the Rocky Mountain states, and white-winged juncos are limited to the Black Hills and scattered locations on the Great Plains to New Mexico and Arizona.

All the juncos look pretty much alike. They are small sparrow-sized birds that are seed-eaters that forage primarily on the ground, and they all possess a song that is a musical trill on a single pitch. Calls differ only slightly. According to the National Geographic *Field Guide to Birds of North America*, dark-eyed junco calls "include a sharp *dit* and, in flight, a rapid twittering." Calls of yellow-eyed birds "include a high, thin *seep*, similar to call of chipping sparrow."

Steve Howell and Sophie Webb provided an additional description of their voice in *A Guide to the Birds of Mexico and Northern Central America*:

A high, sharp, often smacking *tsik* or *sik*, and high, sharp twittering. Song a varied series of bright chips, often with trills or buzzes thrown in, typically the last note rising or up-slurred: *swi swi see-i-ewi'*, or *si-si-si-si-si-si-si-si-ssiu*, or *chiwee chiwee chiwee chiwee chiwee* or *chee-chee zzhi-zzhi zzhi-*zzhi *zzhi-zzhi*, or *we-chu we-chu chi-irrr we shu*, etc.

Although juncos reside in forested areas during the breeding season, both species migrate to lower areas for the winter months. Sometimes all of the western birds can then be found together. Their preferred habitats, according to Howell and Webb, include "pine, pine-oak, and at times oak woodlands with grassy clearings, brush. Feeds on ground and flies up into trees and bushes when flushed. Forms flocks in winter. Sings from prominent perches, often high in trees."

My encounters with yellow-eyed juncos have occur in two very separate locations: Chiricahua National Monument in Arizona and the Maderas del Carmen, the high mountains in Mexico which is located about 50 miles southwest of Big Bend National Park. I wrote about the Chiricahua juncos in *Birding the Southwestern National Parks*, thusly:

Yellow-eyed juncos were present at all elevations, from ground level to the very top of the taller trees, from which they sang melodic, three-part songs with contrasting pitch and rhythm. I located several individuals foraging over the pine needle-clad ground with a strange gait that has been described as a peculiar shuffle, between a hop and a walk. This junco is very different from the wintering dark-eyed juncos that nest in the mountains of central Arizona and northward. Yellow-eyed juncos, earlier known as "Mexican juncos," possess a quiet and calm demeanor, moving over the terrain with leisure, seldom in a hurry. Wintering dark-eyes move in a jerky fashion and seem always to be in a hurry.

In the Maderas del Carmen, I found that montane forest habitat to be very similar to that of the Chiricahuas of southern Arizona. The most numerous bird in the del Carmen highlands was the brown-throated race of the house wren; they seemed to be singing from every pile of downed logs and brush. Next in abundance was the yellow-eyed junco.

I also included yellow-eyed juncos in *A Field Guide to Birds of the Big Bend* as they are a "casual spring visitor." Park records range from March 19 to June 17, and there also is a single fall report in the Chisos Basin on October 26, 1985.

The most recent (2004) Bird List for the park includes yellow-eyed juncos as "acc" in spring and summer.

BOTTERI'S SPARROW

This is a rather plain little dusky-brown bird with a large bill, a flat forehead, long rounded tail, without white tips, whitish breast, and buffy sides. Its back is streaked with brown to rust, and the undersides is gray, often with a yellowish tinge. It is one of those birds that often goes unnoticed. However, it can be located in the right habitat and right time of years by its call notes that are sharp *pit* or *tsip* notes. And the male's song has been described as a jumble of notes; assiduous pitting with some tinkling and churring, often accelerating into a brief rattle, according to Harry Oberholser in *The Bird Life of Texas*. He also mentions that Botteri's sing from "a low perch, often a fence wire, sometimes from the ground." He adds that "Botteri's Sparrow sings from mid-March to late July, occasionally in September."

Steve Howell and Sophie Webb provided another description of its voice *in A Guide to the Birds of Mexico and Northern Central America*: "Song is a varied series of hesitant chips, in full song breaking into a sweet, accelerating or bouncing-ball trill: *ssi, si si-pit sir si, si-pit see seeu weet weet-weewiwiwiwiwiwiwiwi*, etc. Calls include a high, thin, slighty metallic *sik* or *siik*."

Botteri's sparrows are tropical birds that barely enter the United States in the southeastern corner of Arizona and in south Texas. Their essential habitats include arid to semiarid brushy scrub, thorn forest with grassy clearings, savannah and fields with scattered bushes and trees. Oberholser stated that it is an "inhabitant of tall bunchgrass; in Texas it lives mostly within twenty miles of the Gulf of Mexico. Plenty of rank grass, a foot or more tall, growing between widely scattered mesquite and huisache bushes, plus some wild flowers for seeds and occasional low fence wire for perching."

In Mexico, its range extends along the Gulf Slope to the Isthmus, all of the central area of the country, and along the Pacific Slope in a wide band from Arizona to Guatemala. Botteri's sparrows do not occur within the Chihuahuan Desert; they are absent from a huge region of south Texas and north-central Mexico.

At Rancho Nuevo, Tamaulipas, where I spent nine days (May 2-10, 1976) on the beach working with Ridley turtles, I also surveyed the birdlife within five adjacent habitats: littoral scrub, mangroves, thorn scrub, thorn forest, and riparian. I recorded a total of 146 species, 53% of these were breeding, 47% were transients. I recorded 29 Botteri's sparrows in the littoral scrub habitat, 8 within the thorn scrub, and 4 in the thorn forest. None were found in the mangroves and riparian habitats. The littoral shrub occurs between the dunes and the thorn scrub habitat, and varies in width from 65 to 160 feet. The vegetation is dominated by saltwort, sea oxeye, leather-stem, huisache, and bullthorn acacia.

Botteri's sparrows have the special ability to move from place to place to nest in response to local weather conditions. There are only a few sparrows - rufous-winged, Botteri's, Cassin's, and Worthen's sparrows – that follow patterns of precipitation within the inland desert region. In *Birder's Mexico*, I wrote that "they can be expected only in areas that have had adequate moisture, and may be completely absent elsewhere, even though they have been common there the previous year."

Kent Rylander added some additional comments about their behavior in *The Behavior of Texas Birds*. "They forage for insects and seeds by running or hopping on the ground." And he stated that "They flush easily, sometimes flying to a post or other perch, but more often dropping immediately back down into the grass."

I can attest to this habit. While surveying the birdlife of the Norias Division of the King Ranch in South Texas, I recall following a Botteri's sparrow for a considerable distance trying to get a good look; each time I located one it would immediately drop down and fly or run away before I could get an adequate look. And they did not seem to be attracted to low spishing or squeaking sounds. They are very shy birds.

OLIVE SPARROW

This is a large, chunky sparrow that is olive colored above with a whitish underside, a broad brown stripe on each side of its reddish crown, and a narrow black line through each eye. Its song is a "monotonous series of notes: *chip chip chip chip-chip-chip-chipchipchip* which sounds like a small steel ball bouncing to rest on concrete," according to Harry Oberholser, in *The Bird Life of Texas*. Oberholser adds that "it is louder and more metallic than the Field Sparrow's similar vocalization. Singing is chiefly from early March to late July."

And Kent Rylander, in *The Behavior of Texas Birds*, describes its voice, thusly:

> Call: a loud clink, suggesting a Northern Cardinal's call; also, soft ticking notes, probably to maintain contact between individuals. Song: a series of notes terminating in a trill, recalling the Field Sparrow's bouncing ball song pattern, but louder and more metallic.

Actually, the olive sparrow is a tropical species that is native in Mexico to both the Gulf and Pacific Slopes and the northern half of the Yucatan Peninsula. The northernmost edge of its range reaches into the United States only in South Texas from about Del Rio eastward to the Gulf of Mexico. That area includes all of the South Texas brushlands.

Mark Lockwood and Brush Freeman provided a more detailed account of their Texas range in *Handbook of Texas Birds*:

> Common resident throughout the South Texas Brush Country. Olive Sparrows reach the northern limits of their range on the southern edge of the Edwards Plateau where they have a discontinuous distribution, but they are primarily found from central Val Verde County to Uvalde County. Along the Coastal Prairies, they are found north to Refugio County. Olive Sparrows are casual to very rare visitors north to Wilson and Bexar Counties.

I have had personal encounters with olive sparrows in four separate locations: Amistad National Recreation Area near Del Rio; the Norias Division (southeastern quarter) of the King Ranch in South Texas; the Rancho Nuevo area in the central Gulf Coast in Tamaulipas, Mexico; and in northern Yucatan, Mexico.

I included my encounters with olive sparrows at Amistad in *Birding the Southwestern National Parks*, as follows:

I found fifty-two bird species from the roadway in about three hours. Most interesting was the diversity of species within the riparian habitat. For instance, both the western Bullock's Oriole and the eastern Orchard Oriole were present; individuals were chasing one another about the mesquite and huisache in typical oriole courting fashion. Northern Bobwhites, apparently at the western edge of their range, were common there too, delivering their loud "bob-white" calls with great vigor. I also discovered a few Brown-crested Flycatchers and Long-billed Thrashers and numerous Olive Sparrows. These three are Mexican birds that range north only to South Texas and westward along the Rio Grande as far as Amistad.

On the Norias, I discovered that that habitat contained one of the highest biomasses of any study site I have experienced anywhere. Although my main reason for surveying the birds there was to access the population of ferruginous pygmy-owls, I also conducted a number of both walking and driving transects on each of my eight trips. I discovered that the single most common bird was the olive sparrow.

At Rancho Nuevo, during my two-week stay, I established five walking transects to document the area's birdlife. I included details about this project in *My Wild Life, A Memoir of Adventures Within America's National Parks*:

> The transects were located in five distinct habitats: a littoral zone with littoral scrub and mangrove habitats; thorn scrub with either dense vegetation or open in places where grazing occurred; thorn forest where larger trees and shrubs were dominant; and riparian habitat that was more luxuriant and dense due to the continuous presence of ground water.
>
> I recorded 147 bird species within the five habitats: 82 (56%) were nesting and 65 (44%) were migrants…Only 6 of the 82 breeding birds were found to nest in all five habitats: red-billed pigeon, groove-billed ani, ladder-backed woodpecker, Couch's Kingbird, olive sparrow, and Altamira oriole.

Comparative numbers of olive sparrows within the five habitats included 39 individuals in the thorn forest habitat, 38 individuals in the thorn scrub, 18 in the mangrove habitat, 12 in the littoral scrub, and 3 in the riparian habitat. All and all, olive sparrows were the single most abundant bird found at Rancho Nuevo.

My Rancho Nuevo data was later published in an article I wrote for the journal *Cotinga* 10:13-19, 1999: Avian population survey of a Tamaulipan scrub habitat, Tamaulipas, Mexico.

I also recorded olive sparrows in the Yucatan. Although their numbers there did not come close to their abundance in central Tamaulipas, I did find a few individuals at three different locations during my visit there during January 15 to 27, 1978; all within the thorn scrub habitats near Chichén Itza, Cobá, and Milágros.

PYRRHULOXIA

The pyrrhuloxia truly is an arid-land bird. It is found only in the Sonoran and Chihuahuan Deserts of the Southwestern United States and adjacent Mexico. Its scientific name is *Cardinalis sinuous*. Gary Clark, in *Book of Texas Birds*, stated that its common name "combines Pyrrhula, meaning "flame colored," and loxia derived from a word meaning "crooked." So, the strange name gives us "flame-colored bird with a crooked beak," not a peaceably descriptive moniker."

The pyrrhuloxia closely resembles the northern cardinal but lacks the male cardinal's all-red body and bill. Both sexes of pyrrhuloxias have yellow bills. Males are a subtle buff color with a red face and throat and with red on the tip of the crest, belly, and tail. Females are duller, but in the right sunlight, they can show a golden hue. Pyrrhuloxias possess a clear "quink" call, all on the same pitch, while the cardinal's call is a slurred whistle, like "cheer" notes. Pyrrhuloxia calls are thinner and shorter.

Pyrrhuloxia vocalizations have been described by various authors. National Geographic's *Field Guide to the Birds of North America* states that its song is "a liquid whistle, thinner and shorter than the Northern Cardinal's; call is a sharper *chink*." And Kent Rylander, in *The Behavior of Texas Birds*, wrote: "Voice. Call: an abrupt, metallic *cheek*, much like the Northern Cardinal's, but usually less staccato, *queet queryuuu*, often sung from a conspicuous perch. The male advertises his territory by singing, most intensely in early morning. Apparently, females sing very little."

In spite of pyrrhuloxias rating second in avian beauty contests to cardinals, they do possess a subtle beauty. John O'Neill understood that beauty when he painted the pair of pyrrhuloxias that appear in *John O'Neill Great Texas Birds*. Holly Carver wrote the adjoining description. She wrote:

> The Pyrrhuloxia encapsulates the less-than-spectacular but nonetheless intense beauty of Texas…Hard to appreciate if you are looking for drama, the Pyrrhuloxia's quiet colors are those of the desert at dawn, of the one neon sign glowing along Rio Grande City's empty main street. Like the Valley itself, the Pyrrhuloxia reveals little at first glance. But only those who take the time for a second glance discover this bird's appeal.

The majority of my encounters with pyrrhuloxias occurred during the years that I worked at Big Bend National Park. In *A Field Guide to the Birds of the Big Bend*, I wrote the following:

> Pyrrhuloxia *Cardinalis siniatus* Common summer and winter resident; uncommon migrant. This is the bird of desert washes; the look-alike Northern Cardinal prefers riparian areas. Pyrrhuloxias can usually be found at mesquite-acacia thickets along the drier parts of the floodplain and in arroyos and canyons up to 4,500 feet. Lowland birds are mostly permanent

residents. Nesting occurs in April, May, and June; I found adults feeding young at Rio Grande Village on May 21, 1968, and a nest seven feet up in a mesquite there on June 14, 1968. Pyrrhuloxias are fairly shy while nesting but become easy to find again right afterward. Except among the resident birds of the floodplain, there appears to be considerable wandering after nesting. These birds become quite numerous at Panther Junction and in the Chisos Basin during late July and August. By October, birds may be found in the higher parts of the mountains as well; I saw two in upper Boot Canyon on October 22, 1967, and one near the South Rim on November 4, 1967. Wintering records are all below 5,000 feet. Many resident birds congregate in flocks of ten to thirty birds from late September through the first of March. Those in the lower mountain canyons flock, but are usually found in groups of three or four.

In *The Bird Life of Texas*, Harry Oberholser included a paragraph on nesting, as follows:

Nest: On flatland, mesas, and in valleys; in thickets and brush, sometimes isolated; in thorny bush, mesquite, or other low trees, from 3 to 8 ft. above ground; rather large, compact cup; composed of strips of bark, thin and coarse grasses, and twigs; lined with rootlets, fine grasses, and other vegetable fibers. *Eggs*: 3-4 usually 4; ovate to nearly oval; white; dotted and blotched over entire surface, but more so at large end, with umber, other shades of dark brown, and shell markings of purplish gray.

In Texas, based on data in *Birding Texas*, by Roland Wauer and Mark Elwonger, pyrrhuloxias are resident in six of the ten regions of the state. They are most common in the Trans-Pecos, Brush Country, and the Rio Grande Valley. They are fairly common on the Edwards Plateau and Coastal Bend. Occasional birds are reported for the Panhandle and Western Plains, Northern Plains, and Upper Coast. On the Central Plains, they are considered uncommon winter visitors only. There are no records for the Pineywoods region in East Texas.

Oberholser wrote about the behavior of pyrrhuloxias, thusly:

Thornbush dweller is similar to the Cardinal in its behavior. Movement is largely restricted to brief, noisy fluttering amid bushes and trees. Through well camouflaged in its arid haunts, the Pyrrhuloxia often seems reluctant to show itself when a bird watcher squeaks. Most feeding is done on the ground; however, the species forages in vegetation perhaps somewhat more than the Cardinal. The Pyrrhuloxia diet includes seeds of bristlegrass, doveweed, sandbur, panicum, sorghum, pigweed, and others; fruit of cactus and nightshade; also, such insects as grasshoppers, caterpillars, beetles, stinkbugs, and cicadas.

Rylander also commented on their feeding habitats: "like Northern Cardinals, they hop on the ground or in low vegetation while foraging for insects, seeds, and berries, but they spend less time on the ground than Northern Cardinals."

In Mexico, where it is known as *Cardenal Desértico*, pyrrhuloxias are common to fairly common residents throughout the Sonoran and Chihuahuan Deserts, almost to Mexico City. In late April, 1977, I spent five days surveying the birdlife along the central Gulf Coast of Sonora, between Bahia Kin and Desemboque (the northernmost Seri village). I was accompanied by Elsie and Joe Marshall and Dick Russell. Three distinct habitats were surveyed: littoral scrub, desertscrub, and thornscrub. Although I recorded pyrrhuloxias in both the desertscrub and thornscrub habitats, I found no evidence of nesting. I believed those birds were winter residents only.

However, in May 1982, Bo and Woody West and I found pyrrhuloxias in the thorn-scrub habitat just northwest of Mazatlán, Sinaloa, and after crossing the Gulf of Mexico to La Paz, and driving south into Southern Baja to San Bartolo, we found pyrrhuloxias in the desert there below the Sierra de San Lazaro, as well. Those birds undoubtedly were nesting in both areas at the time.

Except for the ubiquitous verdins and black-throated sparrows, few other birds represent America's desert landscapes as does the pyrrhuloxia. After spending six years in Big Bend, it was one of the few birds that I missed after leaving the desert.

VARIED BUNTING

My favorite bunting is the varied bunting, probably because I have spent the most amount of time with this beautiful creature. It is one of the avian specialties of Big Bend National Park. I worked there as Chief Park Naturalist from 1966 to 1972. I included the varied bunting in my chapter on the birds of Big Bend in *The Visitor's Guide to the Birds of the Rocky Mountain National Parks*, thusly:

> The varied bunting is a contender for the park's most beautiful bird. Although its beauty is subtle, compared with some warblers and the closely related painted bunting of the Rio Grande floodplain, the varied bunting's purplish body, red nape and throat, and bluish rump make it truly spectacular in good light. An earlier name for this bird, and well-deserved, was "beautiful" bunting. It is another Mexican species that visits the southern border area of the United States only in summer. It frequents the brushy grasslands but occurs between the desert and the Chisos woodlands. During years with heavy or average rainfall, this bird can be found in surprising abundance, but it can be uncommon during dry years. The best locations to find this bird include Blue Creek Canyon above the old ranch buildings, lower Green Gulch, and along the Window Trail.

An additional description of this beautiful bird was provided by Steve Howell and Sophie Webb in *A Guide to the Birds of Mexico and Northern Central America*:

> It looks blackish with some but not all areas of varied colors and catching the light. Black lores and chin contrast with violet-blue face, nape reddish with

violet-blue hindcollar. Back dark reddish, rump violet-blue; wings and tail black, edged bluish. Throat and chest dark reddish becoming deep purple on belly and undertail coverts. Head and body heavily veiled buffy in fresh basic.

The voice of the varied bunting was described by Harry Oberholser in *The Bird Life of Texas* as "a thin, crisp, energetic warbling similar to that of the Painted Bunting, but more obviously phrased and less rambling. The male, from atop a bush of yucca stalk, sometimes a high wire, sings from mid-April to July. The call is a thin *chirp chirp*."

I included additional details about varied buntings at Big Bend in *A Field Guide to Birds of the Big Bend*:

Varied Bunting. *Passerina versicolor*. Fairly common summer resident and spring migrant. The earliest spring records include an adult male seen at Rio Grande Village on April 4, 1972, and one caught in a mist net at Panther Junction on April 18, 1969; it was banded and released. During the first two weeks of May, Varied Buntings become fairly common over the desert, particularly along the roadsides. Males apparently arrive on their breeding grounds first and are later followed by the females; on April 29, 1970, I found four singing males along the Window Trail, but no females. A male was actively defending a territory in this same area on May 24, and a male was seen feeding two youngsters there on July 19.

I found a nest with three young in Blue Creek Canyon on June 4, and seven singing males within one mile of Cottonwood Wash, just behind the Old Sam Nail Ranch, on July 13. Four singing males and one nest on a squawbush were found along one mile of Blue Creek Canyon, just above the Wilson Ranch House, on June 4. It also can be found in summer in a little wash below Government Spring, and on June 5, I found four singing birds among the mesquite thickets north of the roadway northeast of Todd Hill.

There seems to be double-brooding or late nesting as well. I found an adult male feeding two fledged birds along the Window Trail on August 28, 1966; and on August 23, 1970, I found nine singing males and several females and immature birds along a two-mile stretch of lower Panther Canyon. A visit there on September 13 turned up only two adult males, but one was feeding three very recently fledged youngsters.

There appears to be some post-nesting wandering along the washes, but the bird can usually be found with some searching in the proper habitat until mid-September. In winter, it has been reported on a number of occasions: below the Basin Campground, at Glenn Spring, and at Santa Elena Canyon.

There is no better place to find this lovely songbird in the United States than Big Bend National Park. However, summertime birds also occur in extreme southeastern Arizona. And breeding varied buntings also occur south of the border within suitable habitats throughout most of the Sonoran and Chihuahuan Deserts.

Preferred habitats of varied buntings were mentioned by Howell and Webb:

"Thorn forest, forest edge, scrubby woodland, overgrown clearings, mainly in arid situations but in winter also humid forest edge. Singly or in small groups; often slightly skulking, on or near ground, at times in canopy of fruiting trees."

One characteristic of the U.S. buntings is that all are neotropical migrants. The vast majority migrate southward immediately after their breeding season. Most spread out all across Mexico, although the varied bunting overwinters just below its breeding grounds, but north of the Isthmus. Lazuli bunting winters primarily in the western half of the country, and the indigo bunting spends its wintertime even further south, from central Mexico south to Honduras.

WHITE-COLLARED SEEDEATER

This tiny black-and-white bird is a breeding bird in the United States, although its U.S. range is limited to an area along the Rio Grande from about Laredo east to near Boca Chica. Mark Lockwood and Brush Freeman included further details about its range in *Handbook of Texas Birds*. They stated that it is an:

> Uncommon to rare resident along the Rio Grande from Starr County north through Webb County. White-collared Seedeaters have been reported irregularly east to Hidalgo County. There is also a recent report from Kenedy County near Quemado, Maverick County, on 4 May 2002. This species was more widespread in the Lower Rio Grande Valley but was virtually extirpated from the United States in the late 1950s and early 1960s, as much of its habitat was converted to croplands. It has been suggested that the decline was closely tied to the heavy use of herbicides and pesticides, including DDT.

Preferred habitats of white-collared seedeaters were described by Timothy Brush in *Nesting Birds of a Tropical Frontier*:

> Seedeaters readily use pastures and roadsides, with low grass and scattered trees and shrubs, in moist tropical areas. In drier South Texas, seedeaters appear more restricted to areas near water, because this is where their habitat is. In Hidalgo County, seedeaters were once fairly common in open floodplain forests of black willow. These areas were regularly flooded, and grass and other herbaceous plants sprang up as the water receded. Currently

[2005] seedeaters are seen mainly in areas with common reed or giant reed, adjacent to low meadows with shorter grasses.

Male white-colored seedeaters possess contrasting plumage. Their cap is blackish with a broad white collar that extends from the pure white throat in an upward crescent to its neck. Its back is black-brown with two white wing bars. Females are overall brown with two white wing bars and a white patch at the base of the primaries.

Seedeater's song is high-pitched and sweet, and its call is like a high-pitched "wink." Kent Rylander, in *The Behavior of Texas Birds*, described its song as "a loud and clear *sweet sweet sweet cheer cheer*, suggesting an Indigo Bunting, and notably loud for the size of the bird."

Another description of its voice was provided by Steve Howell and Sophie Webb in *A Guide to the Birds of Mexico and Northern Central America*: "A nasal cheh or *nyek*, and a clear slightly piercing, often quite loud *seeu*, suggesting a euphonia. Song a characteristic sound of open country on both slopes, especially in summer: a varied sweet warble, often speeding into a buzzy trill."

South of the border, its range extends in a wide band along the lower Gulf and Pacific Slopes of Mexico to Honduras and Nicaragua. I have recorded this bird at weedy patches numerous times. I wrote about one incident near a swampy area along the highway on a 1974 Christmas Bird Count near Catemaco, Mexico, in *Birder's Mexico*:

> The most abundant bird there was the gray-crowned yellowthroat, but I also found several white-collared seedeaters and blue-black grassquits... As darkness began to settle into the lowlands, just when it was almost impossible to see across the swamp, a large brownish-streaked bird, with a long bill and legs, suddenly flew up and away: a limpkin. Apparently, it had been there all along, feeding in the tall grass within one hundred or so feet from where I was standing, although I had not seen it.

My attention that day had been concentrating on the dozen or so white-collared seedeaters that I was counting along the roadside.

Another memory of white-collared seedeaters is from one early morning at Francisco Escarega in southern Mexico. While waiting for an Aerovias flight to Tikal, we walked along the edge of the runway, checking out what birds might be present. The most numerous birds found in that rather arid surroundings that morning was an amazing number of white-collared seedeaters.

COLIMA WARBLER

The song came from the oaks over the trail ahead. It was a rapid series of melodic chips that ascended slightly and ended in a sharp tic note. It came again, lasting not more than two or perhaps three seconds. Then silence, except for the other nearby bird songs. I walked slowly along the trail to where I was much closer to where I had heard the song, to where I could see movement among the oak leaves just ahead. And then, almost on cue, it sang again. And there, among the deep green oak leaves, was a gray and yellow Colima warbler, the bird of my search. As I watched, it put its head back and sang again, a spirited song that, to me, represented the essence of Big Bend National Park and the Chisos Mountains.

That initial experience with the Colima warbler occurred many years ago, even before I was assigned to Big Bend National Park as Chief Park Naturalist in 1966. It was my first sighting of one of the most wanted of North America's birds, a "specialty bird" that birders travel from all parts of the country, even many parts of the world to see.

Until 1928, the Colima warbler was a Mexican species only, known only from a handful of specimens. The first of these came from the state of Colima in 1889 – hence its name – and utilized in the initial description by Outram Bangs in 1925. Frederick M. Gaige of the University of Michigan expanded the bird's range into the United States in 1928, when he collected one in the Chisos Mountains of Texas. Since then it has been recorded there regularly, although it has never been found to nest elsewhere in the United States. The Colima warbler and Big Bend's Chisos Mountains have become synonymous.

The first scientific name used by Bangs in his initial description was *Vermivora crissalis*, but the genus name was later changed to *Halminthophila*, and it was changed again to *Leiothlygis*, and a third time to *Oreothlypis*. However, the majority of bird books still use *Vermivora*. At least nine North American warblers fall into the *Vermivora* genus. These include blue-winged, golden-winged, Tennessee, orange-crowned, Bachman's, Nashville, Virginia's, and Lucy's. The later three species are most similar to the Colima, in general appearance and song. In fact, some ornithologists claim that Colimas and Virginia's interbreed. The Virginia's warbler migrates through the Big Bend region and nests in the Rocky Mountains as far south as the Davis Mountains in West Texas, only about 150 miles north of the Chisos Mountains. It differs from the Colima by possessing a yellowish instead of a gray chest, and a smaller bill.

The Colima warbler is a relatively large warbler (4.5-5 inches in length from bill to the end of the tail) with a heavy bill (for a warbler), snow-white eye rings, brownish-gray plumage with a yellowish rump and under tail coverts, and a reddish crown patch. Its spring plumage, especially a territorial male singing in the sunshine from an oak in Boot Canyon, is truly a lovely creature. From below, its gray chest that contrasts with its dull yellow flanks and bright yellow crissum is unique.

Sooner or later, therefore, all active birders will visit the Chisos Mountains to see the Colima warbler. But it is not an easy bird to find. Besides the extensive travel often necessary even to reach West Texas, the Chisos Mountains, the centerpiece of Big Bend National Park, is more than 100 miles south of the nearest major highway (US 90). And then, once one enters the national park and drives into the Chisos Basin, one must hike at least three miles into the Pinnacles or to Boot Canyon, a nine-mile round-trip hike, to find a Colima warbler. The Pinnacles Trail is the nearest but steepest route; it climbs about 1,800 feet in three miles.

Boot Canyon is the heart of the Chisos Mountains. This moist highland drainage lies along the southern edge of Emory Peak, the park's high point at 7,835 feet elevation, and runs for about two miles from the South Rim (7,200 ft.) to the Boot Canyon "pouroff" into upper Juniper Canyon. Boot Canyon is dominated by Arizona cypress and Arizona pine, with an understory of Emory and Grave's oaks and mountain maples. Mexican pinyons, alligator and drooping junipers, gray oaks, and Texas madrones dominate the adjacent slopes.

During most years, Boot Canyon and its side-canyons support up to 35 pairs of Colima warblers in spring and summer. Several other areas in the Chisos are utilized by smaller numbers of breeding Colimas. For instance, the oak-maple canyons along the north sides of Emory Peak, such as below Laguna Meadow and along the Pinnacles Trail, support nesting birds most years. Birds also usually can be found in upper Pine Canyon, on the eastern side of the mountains, and accessible by an eight-mile backcountry road and a two-mile hike. And at least since 1995, a dozen of more pairs of Colimas have utilized a high north-facing slope in upper Green Gulch.

Associated birds of interest to visiting birders within the Colima warbler's preferred environment include blue-throated and broad-tailed hummingbirds, acorn and ladder-backed woodpeckers; Cordilleran and ash-throated flycatchers; Hutton's vireo; Mexican jay; violet-green swallow; bushtit; Bewick's, canyon, and rock wrens; painted redstart (some years); black-headed grosbeak; and hepatic tanager.

All the *Vermivora* warblers (except for Lucy's) are ground-nesters. Colimas construct their nests of grasses and hair along a gradual slope, usually well hidden among the grasses or under a root or rocky outcropping. Adjacent woody vegetation provides natural stair-steps for arriving and leaving the nests, as well as adding protection from predators or accidental damage from passing hikers. Occasionally a nest is built so close to the trail that a birder can peak into the nest without ever leaving the trail.

One of America's Neotropical migrants, that winters in southwestern Mexico and nests in the U.S., Colimas arrive on their Chisos Mountains breeding grounds during March and April. The earliest sighting is March 18. But much depends upon the availability of caterpillars and various other insects among the early leafing oaks. Tiny green oak caterpillars are especially important as a diet for the nestlings. Colimas forage primarily in the upper foliage but also seek insects in the undergrowth.

If adequate food is available, males immediately select a territory and begin to defend those areas from other Colimas. Although their singing is most vigorous during the morning and evening hours, a territorial male will often sing throughout the day as it feeds and courts its mate among the oaks and maples. Both sexes share duties during the nest-building stage as well as during incubation and feeding of the young. Early fledglings may be out and about by mid-May, although late nesters, due to a late season or early nest destruction, may not produce young until July or even August. Early departures can occur as early as August, but Colimas have been found on the breeding grounds as late as September 19.

The Chisos Mountains of Big Bend National Park are the northern tip of the Colima's breeding range that extends southward into the Mexican states of Coahuila, San Louis Potosi, and southwestern Tamaulipas. Essential habitats within various mountain ranges are similar, all at mid-elevations and dominated by oaks and maples with adjacent pines, junipers and madrones. Shrubs, grasses, and succulents (agave and cacti) are present in the understory. The majority of the Mexican range is even less accessible than that in the Chisos Mountains, making the West Texas birds the best bet for most birders.

Because Colimas breed nowhere else in the United States, and since the population there is subject to various catastrophes, such as wildfires, deep drought, and various other threats, it was considered for listing as endangered in 1967. The International Union for Conservation of Nature already listed the Colima as "near threatened," because of its "small U.S. population," and found only in the extremely northern edge of its range. I found that listing totally unnecessary and fruitless. To ward off that action, I initiated a survey of breeding Colimas to prove that they were common in the Chisos and also to provide an adequate baseline to allow for long-term monitoring of the populations.

That first year, I asked help from several birding friends – Jon Barlow, James Dick, Ned Fritz, John Galley, Wes Hetrick, Ted Jones, Jim Lane, Anne LeSassier, Dick Nelson, Mike Parmeter, Kent Rylander, and Francis Williams - and I set the date to correspond to what I had found to be the peak of the Colimas' breeding cycle, the second week of May. I selected twelve areas in the Chisos Mountains to be surveyed. The twelve areas included Upper, Middle and Lower Boot Canyon, East Rim Canyon, the South Rim Trail, Mt. Emory Trail, Laguna Meadow Canyon, the Southeast Corner of the Chisos Basin, Pine and Maple Canyon, and Kibby Spring. Totals for the first (1967) was 46 individuals. In 1968, 65 individuals were counted, 83 in 1969, and 59 in 1970. I then skipped three years, but undertook counts within the same locations in 1974 and 1976. In 1974, 48 were counted and 52 were found in 1976.

I later analyzed all of my data and found that the Colima warbler population in the Chisos seemed to be in a direct correlation to the amount of precipitation during the breeding season of the previous year. I was able to demonstrate that the Colima population in the Chisos was stable and viable. Being in a national park, where full protection from habitat degradation was constant, listing as endangered or even threatened was unnecessary.

TROPICAL PARULA

The tropical parula is a widespread and common bird in the tropics, but it is a rare or uncommon bird in the United States; it is found only in South Texas. Breeding birds have been reported only in the Lower Rio Grande Valley in Webb, Hidalgo and Willacy Counties and north along the Gulf Coast to Brooks and Kenedy Counties. Mark Lockwood and Brush Freeman, in *Handbook of Texas Birds*, wrote that "Tropical Parulas are most common in the live oak woodlands of the Coastal Sand Plain in Kenedy and Brooks Counties. They are rare and local summer residents north along the coast to Calhoun and Victoria Counties."

Tropical parulas, also known as olive-backed, Sennett's, and Pitiayumi warblers, are small, boldly patterned, short-tailed warblers that are distinguished by a dark gray-blue cap and wings with two white wing-bars, olive back, and yellow undersides. Their bright yellow chest, however, contains a broad reddish wash. Their bill is exceedingly sharp, black above and yellow below, and they lack the partial white eye-ring of their northern cousin. Although their plumage shows more contrast than that of the northern parula, their voices are very similar.

Steve Howell and Phoebe Webb provided a description of their voice in *A Guide to the Birds of Mexico and Northern Central America*: "A sharp *chik*, much like Northern Parula. Song variable. A varied arrangement of high, thin buzzes and chips, at times accelerating into a rapid trill or ending abruptly with an upward-inflected note, *syi-syi-syi-syi-syi-syi sisistsiiiiirr, e*tc."

Migrants normally arrive in the U.S. in mid-March and frequent mossy woodlands with oak, Mexican ash, and sugar hackberry trees, usually draped with Spanish and/or ball moss. Harry Oberholser, in *The Bird Life of Texas*, wrote:

> It is a bird of the woods, dense or open, and undergrowth, brush, and trees along the edge of rivers and resacas. It remains much in upper branches of trees and in places is sometimes very common. Although scarcely to be called gregarious, it may be seen at times in small companies of three or more.... Nests, built by the female, are often located toward the end of a branch."

During the years that I visited the Norias, the southeastern quarter of the 400,000-acre King Ranch, to access the population of ferruginous pygmy-owls, I also surveyed all of the area's birdlife. I later published my findings – titled "The Ferruginous Pygmy-Owl in South Texas" - in *American Birds*.

During the more than 20 visits to the Norias, I recorded several bird species that are considered South Texas specialties. Examples include plain chachalaca, ferruginous pygmy-owl, common pauraque, northern beardless-tyrannulet, tropical parula, Audubon's oriole, and olive sparrow. Although the chachalaca, pygmy-owl, pauraque, oriole, and sparrow were widespread over the ranch, tyrannulets and tropical parulas were found only at oak mottes that contained the "mossy" character mentioned above. The Tate Mill site, within the Badéno Pasture, is one example. I found nesting tropical parulas utilizing the relatively tall oaks and hackberries that owed their existence to available water pumped by a windmill into an overflowing basin for cattle.

Timothy Brush, in *Nesting Birds of a Tropical Frontier*, mentions its feeding behavior, thusly:

> The Tropical Parula is apparently mainly a stationary gleaner, like the Northern Beardless-Tyrannulet. I have occasionally seen one hover-gleaning (gleaning from a hovering position) or sally-gleaning (flying down to the ground) to get a caterpillar that had fallen or let itself down by a thread to avoid predation. Foraging heights in the Valley usually range from 20 to 35 feet above the

ground. Birds forage on occasion in mesquite, acacia, or other smaller trees in thorn forest, despite their general restriction to tall riparian forest.

Brush also mentions wintering bird behavior: "Wintering individuals may join mixed species flocks (which may contain a Northern Parula) or forage on their own. Once I saw a singing male fly to the ground and bathe in a puddle left by irrigation – under such circumstance I had a good chance to see the olive-yellow patch on the upper back, which is often difficult to see."

In Mexico, tropical parulas occur primarily along the Gulf and Pacific Slopes, missing entirely from the central portion of the country. They also are found in Central America and south to Peru and northern Argentina. Their preferred tropical habitats are similar to those in the north.

Although I have recorded the species numerous times in Mexico, I was able to quantify a population only at Rancho Nuevo, a coastal area in central Tamaulipas. During a two-week stay to study Ridley turtles, I established an avian population survey that included five habitats: littoral scrub, mangroves, thorn scrub, thorn forest, and riparian. Total numbers of species recorded included 535 individuals of 55 species in the thorn forest, 532 individuals of 39 species in the thorn scrub, 524 individuals of 45 species in the riparian, 306 individuals of 26 species in the mangroves, and 218 individuals of 15 species in the littoral scrub zone. I recorded 20 tropical parulas, but were found only in the thorn scrub habitat.

I also wrote about tropical parulas that I found near Mazatlán in *Birder's Mexico*:

We located the calling ferruginous pygmy-owl in a leafless oak tree growing alongside one of the evergreen netleaf oaks in the canyon bottom. For more than twenty minutes we sat nearby and watched other birds mob the pygmy-owl...The most aggressive of the avian mobbers had been one of the smallest, the golden vireo. A pair of these birds had soundly scolded the pygmy-owl from the nearby oak foliage, and remained there in defiance until the owl departed. A lone sulphur-bellied flycatcher seemed to be bravest and actually flew close enough to make the owl, which is just the same size as the flycatcher, duck its head with each pass. A blue mockingbird scolded from the oak foliage, and two or three tropical parulas flitted nervously about. They were joined by a lone rufous-capped warbler.

RED-FACED WARBLER

What an unusual bird is the red-faced warbler. Although its body, with an all-gray back and wings, with one short, whitish wing bar, and white undersides, is nothing special, its head is spectacular! Its entire face and upper throat are bright red, its cap is coal-black, and it has a small white spot on the back of its head.

Its voice is a full chip or *tchip*, and its song is "a sweet warbled series, *wi tsi-wi tsi-wi, si-wi-si-wichu*, and variation," according to Steve Howell and Sophie Webb in *A Guide to the Birds of Mexico and Northern Central America*.

Like a number of other tropical songbirds, red-faced warblers occur as a breeding bird in the United States only in the mountains of southern Arizona and the southwestern corner of New Mexico. These upland areas are the northern extension of Mexico's Sierra Madre Occidental. Their U.S. breeding sites are limited to these Madean sky-islands, namely the uplands of the Santa Ritas, within Coronado National Forest, about 25 miles southeast of Tucson.

Preferred habitats for red-faced warblers occur in pine and aspen forests with deciduous vegetation surrounded by conifer forest, usually between 6,600- and 9,800-feet elevation. Nests, small cups constructed of leaves, grass, and pine needles, are hidden in the ground amid debris, and sheltered under a shrub, log or rock.

In winter, red-faced warblers are found in Mexico, from Sinaloa and Durango to Chiapas, Veracruz, and to Guatemala.

My encounters with this colorful bird occurred in Madera Canyon in the Santa Ritas. I stayed a couple nights in a cabin at Santa Rita lodge and hiked up-canyon into the higher forest from there. I recall locating two individual red-faced warblers a couple miles above the lodge and watching them feed in the foliage of oak trees. I had read about their quirky habit of flicking their tail while feeding, and so I watched it flicking its tail sideways while capturing caterpillars.

Red-faced warblers have also been recorded a few times in Texas. Its presence in the Trans-Pecos region was mentioned by Mark Lockwood and Brush Freeman in *Handbook of Texas Birds*: "Red-faced Warbler *Cardellina rubrifrons.* Very rare late summer and fall migrant to the Chisos Maintains in the Trans-Pecos. Red-faced Warbler is an accidental visitor elsewhere in the state."

I provided additional details about its appearance in the Trans-Pecos in *A Field Guide to the Birds of the Big Bend,* thusly:

> The distribution and status of this brightly marked warbler was documented by Greg Lasley, Dave Easterla, Chuck Sexton, and Dominic Bartol in a comprehensive 1982 article in the *Bulletin of the Texas Ornithological Society*; which is worth reading. They point out that the species nests in the Sacramento and Sandia mountains of New Mexico and that the Big Bend records likely are migrants. However, its presence in the Chisos should be carefully monitored. Because the habitat in the Chisos Mountains appears similar to that on its known breeding grounds in New Mexico; increasing records may suggest an eastern movement of its breeding range.

The possibility of the red-faced warbler being a "regular" migrant through the Big Bend area is questionable. It does not occur in Mexico's Sierra Madre Oriental, the mountain range below the Big Bend area, but it is a fairly common to common breeding bird in the highlands of the Sierra Madre Occidental, directly below Arizona and New Mexico. Howell and Webb state that it is a "breeder on Pacific Slope and in adjacent interior from Son to Dgo...F and U transient and winter visitor (Aug.-Apr) on Pacific Slope from Sin, and interior from cen Mexico, to W Honduras and El Salvador."

Howell and Webb also include a summary of its Mexican habitat, that is similar to that in the U.S., thusly: "Arid to semiarid pine-oak, and oak woodland, in winter also humid pine-evergreen forest and semideciduous woodland. Singly or in pairs at mid- to upper levels, tail often cocked and swung about loosely like Wilson's Warbler; joins mixed-species flocks."

RUFOUS-CAPPED WARBLER

The rufous-capped warbler is an active little warbler that frequents open brushy areas and woodlands at middle elevations in Mexico and southward into Central America. It is distinctly marked with a chestnut crown and cheeks, white eyelines, and a yellow throat and chest. It is a bird that is difficult to mistake.

It also possesses a rather distinct voice. Steve Howell and Sophie Webb described its voice in *A Guide to the Birds of Mexico and Northern Central America* as "A hard chik or *chuk*, often run into an excited rapid chipping series; also, a quiet, high *tsi* or *tik*. Song a rapid, often accelerating, series of chips which may run into a trill, *chi-chi-chi-chi-chi-ssiu-ssiu-ssiu-ssiu*, and variations, often with longer more trilled series."

In spite of its Mexican affinity, there are more than a dozen records north of the border. In Texas, The National Geography bird guide states that it is "casual to Edward's Plateau and Big Bend, Texas; also, southeastern Arizona." And Jim Peterson and Barry Zimmer, in *Birds of the Trans Pecos*, wrote in 1998 that it is "Casual, usually in winter or spring. The seven total records in the Trans-Pecos include four from Big Bend National Park, one from Seminole Canyon State Park...There are two accepted records from Dolan Creek in Val Verde County." They further stated that "Many of these birds stayed for long periods of time, with one bird in Big Bend reported continuously from September 9, 1973, through June 29, 1974."

I discussed the Big Bend records in *A Field Guide to the Birds of the Big Bend* (1996):

Rufous-capped Warbler. *Basileuterus rufifrons*. Sporadic visitor. This little Mexican warbler was first discovered by David Wolf in Campground Canyon on Pulliam Ridge, across from the Chisos Basin campground on September 9, 1973. It was found again in the same location in May 1974… There were numerous reports during June and July…In 1975, it was recorded in Campground Canyon during July and August, and as late as November 25…Then in 1976, it was discovered along the SEC [Santa Elena Canyon] nature trail on August 3.

I wrote about the finding it in Campground Canyon in 1974 in *For All Seasons, A Big Bend Journal*, thusly:

May 24 (1974). Rose Ann Rowlett, Byron Berger, Jerry and Nancy Strickland, and I climbed the steep slope into Campground Canyon this morning to try to find the elusive rufous-capped warbler. David Wolf had discovered it there first on September 9, 1973, but it had disappeared immediately afterward. It was not reported again until May 1974. Now, we slowly worked our way into the narrow canyon, carefully watching for this rare Mexican visitor. We heard it first, a distinct "tzeo" note from the oak trees ahead on the right. Then suddenly it appeared in the open, gleaning the leaves for insects and in clear view of all of us. We watched it through our binoculars for as long as it remained, and then it moved up-canyon and out of sight. It was a new U.S. bird for us all.

Since 1976, there have been scattered reports in the Chisos Mountains, including several photographs to document its occurrence. I further discussed its general status, thusly:

This is a common Mexican warbler of "open woodlands, brushy hillsides, rarely forests; foothills into mts. (to 7000 ft.)," according to *A Field Guide to Mexican Birds* (Peterson and Chalif 1973). Although I have not found it in the Maderas del Carmen Mountains, 50 miles southeast of the Chisos, I have seen it in the Sierra de Musquiz, less than 100 miles southeast of the Maderas del Carmen, and Mike Braun found 70 in the Fraile Mountains, 45 miles south of Falcon Dam, according to Victor Emanuel.

Howell and Webb wrote that the rufous-capped warbler is a "C to F resident (near SL-3000 m) on both slopes from Son and E NL, and in interior from cen Mexico, to W Guatemala; disjunctly in S Belize." They also included the following description of its habitat: "Scrub, semiopen areas with hedges, scattered bushes, second growth, woodland edges. In pair or singly, close to ground, tail often held cocked near vertical."

There is little doubt that the rufous-capped warbler is common within mid-elevations throughout Mexico. I mentioned my two encounters with this bird in *Birder's Mexico*. Firstly, in writing about the very similar golden-browed warbler at Alta Cima, a small village above Gómez Farias in Tamaulipas, I wrote:

> I never did find golden-brows very high in the vegetation: they were always at lower levels within the shrubs and smaller trees, and always with five or more other golden-brows. Their constant activity and always continuous *zi-zi-zi* calls made them easy to tracks as they moved through the forest. Their most common companions were two or more rufous-capped warblers. Crescent-chested warblers were usually members of the party, as well, but they feed higher in the trees. On one occasion I watched a fan-tailed warbler as it foraged near the ground. Its distinct "tail-fanning" behavior, very much like that of an American redstart, was conspicuous.

On another occasion, above Mazatlán, while searching for tufted jays in the Sierra Madre Occidental, I discovered a ferruginous pygmy-owl that was being mobbed by a flock of birds. I also wrote about that incident in *Birder's Mexico*:

> The most aggressive of the avian mobbers had been one of the smallest, the golden vireo. A pair of these birds had soundly scolded the pygmy-owl from the nearby oak foliage, and remained there in defiance until the owl departed. A lone sulphur-bellied flycatcher seemed to be the bravest and actually flew close enough to make the owl, which is just about the same size as the flycatcher, duck its head with each pass. A blue mockingbird scolded from the oak foliage, and two or three tropical parulas flitted nervously about. They were joined by a lone rufous-capped warbler. A streak-backed oriole came by for a few moments to see what the commotion was all about. It scolded briefly but flew off down the canyon. And all the while a lone male

yellow grosbeak sat in the lower branches of a nearby shrub; I was never sure that it was even aware of the presence of the ferruginous pygmy-owl.

On another trip into Mexico, while driving across the central highlands on Highway 150, I stopped to bird a forested area at about 8,000 feet elevation on the southern ridge of Pico de Orizaba. The reason for exploring that area was to attempt to find a slaty finch; Bill Schaldach had collected one there years earlier, and I was following his directions. Although we failed to find a slaty finch, we did add two Mexican birds to my life list: collared towhee and rufous-capped brush-finch. Plus, we also recorded a number of rufous-capped warblers.

Because the rufous-capped warbler is a common to fairly common resident throughout Mexico's mid-elevations, and often in barely accessible areas to humans, its status is secure. Its presence north of the border, what with changes due to global warming, is likely to increase; its preferred Mexican habitats are likely to move northward. Rufous-caps will surely follow that line of habitats as it moves northward.

MEXICAN CHICKADEE

This little Mexican tit enters the United States only in the Chiricahua Mountains of southeastern Arizona and the Animas Mountains of southwestern New Mexico. It looks very much like the black-capped chickadee of the northern portion of North America, but with gray instead of pinkish flanks. And its voice also differs: Mexican chickadee calls are a husky buzz, while the call of the black-cap is a clear, whistled fee-bee or fee-bec.

Steve Howell and Sophie Webb provide additional descriptions of their voice in *A Guide to the Birds of Mexico and Northern Central America*:

> Varied buzzy and excited twittering calls include a buzzy *dzi-ssi-ssi* or *tssir-irr-r*r and *deshi-chik-i-dit*, a shorter buzzy *chi-pi-tit*, an often loud, nasal scolding, *ssheber-sshehr* or *cheb-cheb*. Song a short clear to slightly blurry warble *ss-chirr-i-chu* or *chis'l chu-wur*, and a rich *chee-lee* or *cheelee*, repeatedly rapidly 4-6 X, etc."

Howell and Webb also mention its habitat as "Arid to semihumid conifer and pine-oak forest." They spend their summers in pine and spruce-fir forests, and normally descend to lower pine-oak forests in winter. Wintering birds often join mixed flocks of bridled titmice, kinglets, nuthatches, and warblers. Groups of chickadees are collectively known as "banditry and dissimulation" of birds.

Mexican chickadee diets include both seeds and insects; they feed mainly by gleaning insects from leaves and bark. But, unlike most chickadees they do not store food.

All chickadees are cavity-nesters; nests are lined with plants down and fur; the female does all the brooding. But both parents participate in "sweeping" the cavity entrance. This is done with crushed insects held in the bill and brushed on the entrance; apparently the chemicals from the crushed insects serve to repel predators. And, when leaving the nest, the female may cover the nestlings with nesting materials.

Most of my encounters with Mexican chickadees in U.S. occurred during various visits to Arizona's Rustler Park in the Chihuahuas. Located in a ponderosa pine community with open parks filled with wildflowers, I remember those visits with fond memories. But another memory of watching birds there was not so enjoyable. The chickadees and other songbirds seemed to insist on singing from the tallest conifers; my neck became sore from looking up all day.

In Mexico, I have recorded Mexican chickadees on numerous occasions, and I have written about three of those encounters in *Birder's Mexico*: in the Oaxaca highlands above Mazatlán, in the Sierra Madre Occidental above Durango, and on the upper slopes of Popocatepetl.

Highway 175 runs north from Oaxaca across the Sierra Madre de Sur. It immediately climbs very steeply up a deep canyon to an open forested plateau, then drops again into a deep valley and up again toward the next ridge, and on and on...I stopped at the first good patch of forest, about twenty-five miles from Oaxaca City, and explored that area for about an hour. Almost immediately I encountered a small flock of dwarf jays, another of Mexico's endemics...I also found in that same patch of forest, white-eared hummingbird, a male mountain trogon perched reasonably close by on a pine, greater pewee, acorn woodpecker, northern flicker, Mexican chickadee, brown-backed solitaire, solitary vireo, Townsend's warbler, and hepatic tanager.

The second area was three hours above Mazatlán in the Sierra Madre Occidental. We left our car along an old roadway that crossed over a forested area to a point where we had an outstanding view of the distant ridges and the canyons below; the site had been recommended as a good place to find tufted jays in a nearby canyon. I included details of that day in *Birding Mexico*:

> The route to the barranca was well marked. It started at kilometer post 200, beside a white stucco building with a corrugated tin roof and with the title of the location painted on the front in large black letters – "Campamento del Control de Prevencion y Cobate de Incedios Forestales" – the local forestry camp.

We discovered that the area behind the forestry building had an old roadway that provided excellent birding. Almost immediately we recorded band-tailed pigeon, hairy woodpecker, masked tityra, greater pewee, pine flycatcher, Steller's jay, Mexican chickadee, blue mockingbird, bridled titmouse, ruby-crowned kinglet, American robin, russet nightingale-thrush, several warblers, rufous-capped brush-finch, and rufous-sided towhee.

The third site was off Highway 190, along the northern edge of Popocatepetl (17,781 feet) that was dominated by Montezuma pine and an understory of coarse grasses. I again included details in *Birder's Mexico*:

> I recorded thirty-nine bird species during a two-hour walk through open forest that reminded me very much of mature ponderosa pine in the southwestern part of the United States. The common to fairly common birds recorded included white-eared hummingbird, Strickland's woodpecker, house (brown-throated) wren, Mexican chickadee, bushtit, white-breasted and pygmy nuthatches, ruby-crowned kinglet, and black-throated green, yellow-rumped, red, and olive warblers.

RUFOUS-BACKED ROBIN

October 23, 1966, will forevermore be special to me! I found a rufous-backed robin at Rio Grande Village in Big Bend National Park. That sighting represented the first for Texas and only the second for the United States; it had been reported in Arizona on one earlier occasion.

I spent the entire morning at Rio Grande Village, birding all of the best locations, recording a total of 54 species. By midmorning I was north of the campground along the line of springs that is now known as the Gambusia Ponds. Several common snipes flew away in typical zigzag fashion, with harsh "skipe" calls, as I approached. A pair of pyrrhuloxias, two or three northern mockingbirds, a Say's phoebe, and a few rock wrens were evident on the dry limestone hillsides above the springs.

I paused in front of a particularly dense area of cordgrass, salt cedar, common buttonbush, and tree tobacco and squeaked with the back of my hand against my lips. A pair of northern cardinals immediately responded, flying into view from the honey mesquites beyond. Sudden movement in the foreground attracted my attention, and I watched as a robin-sized bird flew up from the undergrowth, where it apparently had been drinking or feeding. For a brief second, I thought it was an American robin, but on closer examination through binoculars I could see the bird's rufous back and flanks, which contrasted with the otherwise gray plumage. A rufous-backed robin!

It stayed still, watching me for another eight or ten seconds, and then it dropped back into the foliage. I squeaked it back into view once again, but it was extremely nervous and stayed for only a few seconds before flying into the adjacent mesquites in about the same place the cardinals had appeared. I was unable to find it again.

Two days later I got another very brief glance at the bird in the same locality, but I was unable to take a photograph, although I had brought a camera with a long lens with me. I could not locate it again on several succeeding days. Up until mid-1995, there had been only four "accepted" records of this Mexican bird in Texas: one below Falcon Dam on December 29, 1975; one photographed at Langtry on November 11-18, 1976; one near Fort Davis on February 9, 1992; and a specimen from El Paso on October 27, 1993.

The rufous-backed robin is endemic to Mexico where it also is known as rufous-backed thrush (*Turdus rufopalliatus*). Its Mexican range extends along the Pacific Slope from Sonora to Oaxaca; its occurrence in the United States represents wandering birds only. Other U.S. records may represent escaped caged birds. The Big Bend bird, however, showed no evidence of it ever having been caged. Howell and Webb wrote in *A Guide to the Birds of Mexico and Northern Central America* that "Populations in DF [Mexico City] (2200-2500 m), apparently established in the last 50 years…and Oaxaca City…probably derived from escaped cage birds."

Since 1960, there have been a number of records in Arizona, where it is considered a transient and winter visitor to the southeastern corner of the state. And Bob Behrstock, who lives in southern Arizona, recently told me that rufous-backed robins are "tolerably common in Arizona; they can be expected annually." The Arizona birds, however, can be elusive and hide in dense woods or thickets.

In Mexico, I have recorded rufous-backed robins numerous times. I wrote about several of those occasions in *Birder's Mexico.* One occurred in the Oaxaca highlands along Highway 175 that runs across the Sierra Madre de Sur between Oaxaca and Veracruz:

> One of the available pull-outs was located at the bottom of a rather deep barranca that contained a good habitat of broadleaf vegetation and a trail that followed the bottom for several hundred yards. There I found a fruiting tree that I identified as a hackberry, that was full of feeding birds. I sat at a comfortable distance away and watched what took place. Within less than an hour I had added a couple dozen birds to my trip list. Mexican specialties seen there included sport-crowned woodcreeper, tufted flycatcher, several rufous-backed robins, a pair of Aztec thrushes, rufous-capped nightingale-thrush, crescent-chested and red warblers, chestnut-capped brush-finch, and collared towhee.

Another encounter with rufous-backed robins was on the slopes of Volcán Colima, in the humid pine-oak forest at 9,200 feet elevation. Dick Russell and I had driven up a very dusty and winding logging road to where we camped overnight. I wrote about my findings the following morning:

> I was surprised at the abundance of familiar North America birds that we found during the couple of hours we spent exploring this habitat. I recorded four woodpeckers (acorn, ladder-backed and Strickland's woodpeckers, and northern flicker), greater pewee, dusky-capped flycatcher, Cassin's kingbird, bushtit, brown creeper, solitary and warbling vireos; Nashville, yellow, yellow-rumped, Grace's, and MacGillivray's warblers; indigo bunting, and blue and black-headed grosbeaks. Mexican bird specialties were represented by the russet-crowned motmot, gray-barred and bar-vented wrens, both the rufous-backed and white-throated robins, russet nightingale-thrush,

gray silky-flycatcher, rufous-capped warbler, collared towhee, and yellow grosbeak.

Howell and Webb described the preferred habitat of rufous-backed robins as "Arid to semihumid deciduous and semideciduous forest and edge, plantations, gardens. On ground and low to high in trees and bushes; often flocking in winter."

They also described its voice as "A plaintive, mellow, drawn-out whistle, *cheeoo* or *teeu*u, a faint hard clucking *chuk chuk*...or *chok*..., and a high, thin ssi or *ssit*, mostly in flight. Song a leisurely rich warbling, includes 2-3X repetition of some phrases."

The rufous-backed robin is a common to fairly common resident throughout its range in the tropics. I have found no reports of any change in its status.

REFERENCES

American Ornithologist' Union. 1998. *Check-list of North American Birds*. 7th ed. Washington, D.C.: American Ornithologist' Union.

Bailey, Vernon. 1905. *Biological Survey of Texas*. North American Fauna No. 25, Washington, D.C.

Bangs, Outran. 1925. The history and character of *Vermivora crissalis* (Salvin and Goodman). *Auk* 42: 251-53.

Bent, Arthur Cleveland. 1961. *Life Histories of North American Birds of Prey*. New York: Dover Publications, Inc.

Blake, Emmet Reid. 1949. The nest of the Colima warbler in Texas. *Wilson Bull*. 61:65-67.

_____ 1953. *Birds of Mexico*. Chicago: Univ. Chicago Press.

Brandt, Herbert W. 1940. *Texas Bird Adventures*. Cleveland: Bird Research Foundation.

Brown, Lester, and Dean Amadon. 1968. *Eagles, hawks, and falcons of the world*. London: Country Life books.

Brush, Timothy. 2005. *Nesting Birds of a Tropical Frontier*. College Station: Texas A&M Univ. Press.

Cade. Tom J. 1982. *The Falcons of the World*. Ithaca, New York: Cornell Univ. Press.

Clark, Gary. 2016. *Book of Texas Birds*. College Station: Texas A&M Univ. Press.

Clark, William S., and Brian K. Wheeler. 1987. *A Field Guide to Hawks of North America*. Boston: Houghton Mifflin Co.

De La Torres, Julio. 1990. *Owls: Their Life and Behavior*. New York: Crown Publishers, Inc.

Ehrlich, Paul R., David S. Dobkin, and Dattyl Wheye. 1988. *The Birder's Handbook*. New York: Simon and Shuster, Fireside Book.

Gehlbach, Frederick R. 1987. Natural history sketches, densities, and biomass of breeding birds in evergreen forests of the Rio Grande, Texas, and Rio Corona, Tamaulipas, Mexico. *The Texas Journal of Science* 19 (3): 241-51

Halle, Louis J. 1047. *Spring in Washington*. New York: Harper and Brothers.

Howell, Steve N. G., and Sophie Webb. 1995. *A Guide to the Birds of Mexico and Northern Central America*. Oxford: Oxford Univ. Press.

Johnsgard, Paul A. 1988. *North American Owls*. Washington, D.C.: Smithsonian Inst.

Kuban, Joe F., Jr. 1977. "The Ecological Organization of Hummingbirds in the Chisos Mountains, Big Bend National Park, Texas." Master's Thesis, Univ. Texas at Arlington.

Lasley, Gregory W., et. al. 1982. Documentation of the Red-faced Warbler (*Cardellina trubrifrons*) in Texas and a Review of its Status in Texas and Adjacent Areas. *Bull. Texas Ornithological Soc.*, Vol. 15, Nos 1 & 2:8-14.

Lockwood, Mark W. 2001. *Birds of the Texas Hill Country*. Austin: Univ. Texas Press.

_____ and Brush Freeman. 2004. *Handbook of Texas Birds*. College Station: Texas A&M Univ. Press.

Marshall, Joe T. Jr. 1967. *Parallel Variation in North and Middle American Screech-owls*. Los Angeles, Calif.: Monograph no. 1, Western Foundation for Vertebrate Zoology.

National Geographic Society. 1987. *Field Guide to the Birds of North America*. Washington, D.C.

Oberholser, Harry C., and Edgar R. Kincaid, Jr. 1974. *The Bird Life of Texas*. Austin: Univ. Texas.

O'Neill, John P. 1999. *John P. O'Neill Great Texas Birds*. Ed. Suzanne Winckler. Austin: Univ. Texas Press.

Palmer, Ralph S. 1962. *Handbook of North American Birds*. New Haven: Ct: Yale Univ. Press.

Peterson, Jim, and Barry R. Zimmer. 1998. *Birds of the Trans Pecos*. Austin: Univ. Texas Press.

Peterson, Roger Tory, and Edward L. Chalif. 1973. *A Field Guide to Mexican Birds*. Boston: Houghton Mifflin Co.

Phillips, Allan R. 1942. Notes on the migration of the elf and flammulated screech owls. *Wilson Bull.*,54:132-37.

_____, Joe Marshall, and Gale Monson. 1964. *The Birds of Arizona*. Tucson: Univ. Arizona Press.

Pulich, Warren M., Sr., and Warren M. Pulich, Jr. 1963. The nesting of the Lucifer Hummingbird in the United States. *Auk* 80:370-71.

Rylander, Kent. 2002. *The Behavior of Texas Birds*. Austin: Univ. Texas Press.

Schaldach, William J., Jr. 1963. *The avifauna of Colima and adjacent Jalisco, Mexico*. Los Angeles, Calif.: Proc. Western Found. Vertebrate Zoology.

_____ 1969. Further notes on the avifauna of Colima and adjacent Jalisco, Mexico. *An Inst. Biol. Univ. Nat. Auton. Mexico* 49, See. Zool. (2):299-316.

Scott, Peter E. 1993. A Closer Look: Lucifer Hummingbird. *Birding* 25(4):245-51.

Skutch, Alexander E. 1977. *A Birdwatcher's Adventures in Tropical America*. Austin: Univ. Texas Press.

Snyder, D. E. 1957. A Recent Colima Warbler of the Big Bend. *Audubon Mag.*, 52:84-91.

Snyder, Noel, and Helen Snyder. 1991. Birds of Prey. Natural History and Conservation of North American Raptors. Stillwater, MN: Voyageur Press.

Sutton, George Miksch. 1951. *Mexican Birds: First Impressions*. Norman: Univ. Oklahoma Press.

_____ 1972. *At a Bend in a Mexican river*. New York: Paul S. Erikson.

Tveten, John I. 1993. *The Birds of Texas*. Fredericksburg, Tex.: Shearer Publishing.

Van Tyne, Josselyn. 1929. *The Discovery of the Nest of the Colima Warbler (Vermivora crissalis)*. Misc. Publ., Univ. Of Michigan, No. 33.

Wauer, Roland H. 1967a. Colima Warbler Census in Big Bend's Chisos Mountains. *National Parks Magazine*, Nov., 8-10.

_____ 1967b. First Thick-billed Kingbird Record for Texas. *Southwestern Naturalist* 12 (4): 485-86.

_____ 1968. The Groove-billed Ani in Texas. *Southwestern Naturalist* 13 (4): 452.

_____ 1970. The Occurrence of the Black-vented Oriole, *Icterus wagleri*, in the United States. *Auk* (4): 361-62.

_____ 1971. Ecological Distribution of Birds of the Chisos Mountains. *Southwestern Naturalist* 16:1-29.

_____ 1973. *Birds of Big Bend National Park and Vicinity.* Austin: Univ. Texas Press.

_____1977. Interrelations Between a Harris's Hawk and Badger. *Western Birds*. Vol.: 155.

_____ 1978. Head Start for an Endangered Turtle. *National Parks and Conservation Magazine* 52: 16-20.

_____ 1980. *Naturalist's Big Bend*. College Station: Univ. A&M Univ. Press.

_____1993. *The Visitor's Guide to the Birds of the Rocky Mountain National Parks, United States and Canada*. Santa Fe, NM: John Muir Publications.

_____ 1996a. *A Field Guide to Birds of the Big Bend*. Houston, Texas: Gulf Publ. Co.

_____ 1996b. *A Birder's West Indies, An Island by Island Tour*. Austin: Univ. Texas Press.

_____ 1997a. *Birds of Zion National Park and Vicinity*. Logan: Utah State Univ. Press.

_____1997b. *For All Seasons, A Big Bend Journal*. Austin: Univ. Texas Press.

_____ 1999a. *Birder's Mexico*. College Station: Texas A&M Univ. Press.

_____ 1999b. Avian Population Survey of a Tamaulipan Scrub Habitat, Tamaulipas, Mex., *Cotinga* 10: 13-19.

_____ 2001. *Naturally...South Texas*. Austin: Univ. Texas Press.

_____ 2004. *Birding the Southwestern National Parks*. College Station: Texas A&M Univ. Press.

_____ 2014. *My Wild Life, A Memoir of Adventures within America's National Parks.* Lubbock: Texas Tech Univ. Press.

_____ 2019a. *Ruins to Ruins, From the Mayan Jungle to the Aztec Metropolis*. Bloomington, In: Xlibris.

_____2019b. Songbirds of the West. Bloomington, In: Xlibris

_____ and Dennis L. Carter. 1963. *Birds of Zion National Park and Vicinity*.

Springdale, Utah: Zion Natural History Assoc.

_____ and Mark A. Elwonger. 1998. *Birding Texas*. Helene, Mt.: Falcon Press.

_____ and Carl M. Fleming. 2002. *Naturalist's Big Bend*. College Station: Texas A&M Univ. Press.

_____, Paul Palmer, and Anse Windham. 1997. The Ferruginous Pygmy-Owl in South Texas. *American Birds* (47):1071-1076.

Lightning Source UK Ltd.
Milton Keynes UK
UKHW050946140920
369783UK00002B/5